Nordstjernan Förlag, New York 2009
www.nordstjernan.com

A heck of a life
Copyrigth ©text & photo: Lars-Henrik Ottoson
Editing: Ulf Barslund Mårtensson
Design: Daniel D Berubé-Arbello
Typeface: Anziano, Lisboa; www.fountaintype.com
Cover: The author with President Ronald Reagan
Original Swedish title: *Ett liv utan like*, Nordstjernan Förlag, 2005

ISBN-13: 978-0-9672176-7-3
ISBN-10: 0-9672176-7-9

First English edition. Printed in the USA.

Nordstjernan Förlag
Book Services
P.O. Box 1710
New Canaan CT 06840

A HECK OF A LIFE

A HECK OF A LIFE

JOIN LARS-HENRIK OTTOSON

on an incredible journey. Meet chieftains and presidents, world celebrities and notables, in shackles, shrines and palaces; in the halls of power and the backwoods.

NORDSTJERNAN
Förlag, New York

CONTENT

- 9   There are no ordinary people
- 11   Thank you all...
- 15   The burden of past generations
- 21   Stockholm in those days
- 25   Childhood the early years
- 33   The realities of growing up
- 53   It can happen... and it did!
- 67   London Times 67
- 91   Ford, USA and Hollywood
- 107   From Cape to Cape
- 159   Heading home
- 167   Gorilla Gorilla
- 183   Out of Africa, out of mind
- 191   The Anchor man
- 203   'The Champ' and ABBA
- 217   The Bahamas adventure
- 239   America here I come
- 265   Swedish America
- 269   To be continued...
- 273   People index

LARS-HENRIK OTTOSON

Foreword by the publisher

THERE ARE NO ORDINARY PEOPLE

After maybe a thousand close encounters or interviews and perhaps a couple hundred that actually made a difference, it can safely be confirmed—all people are remarkable, exceptional and amazing. All are ordinarily remarkable, even those who are remarkably ordinary. Then there are those who are somehow something more, who have experienced more, seen so much in so many settings and touched so many lives that their own life turns to a crystal with a thousand facets. They become larger than life or, at least larger than one life.

That's Lars.

Lars Ottoson is that to me, and as the kids call him, Uncle Lars. For the early friends—Sven Nykvist, Ingemar Bergman, Bibi Andersson, Henning Sjöström, Benny Andersson, for natives and Bedouins in Africa or for Gösta Pryzelius and Erland Josephsson, perhaps also for Reagan and the older Bush—he is Lars Henrik. The same goes for the Aktuellt TV audience, the readers of Se or Folket i Bild or ...? I am pretty certain that he did not get the attention of the black shirted Adolf at the Town Hall Square in Hamburg in the 1930s, but if he had, he'd surely have been HERR Ottoson.

I sat poolside at the then Swedish owned Surf and

Sand Hotel in Vero Beach in the late 1980s. The much talked about Lars Ottoson was to meet me there to discuss the possibility of cooperation. As a permanent resident of the south engaged in the work of the Swedish American Chamber of Commerce (which he co-founded), as former editor of the native American newspaper *Alligator Times*, and as a generally well known writer he was important to us at Nordstjernan. From my seat by the pool I could see the parking lot, and five minutes before we agreed to meet a burgundy Jaguar drove up. He exited with shoulder length white hair, wearing a rose colored Lacoste golf shirt, loafers with no socks and white Bermuda shorts.

He looked his life. Expressive, colorful, many-faceted and much like a loosely connected quilt. If his will to discover and experience the joy of living, sometimes the will to survive, had been less profound, everything would have been different.

That is not the case. When you read Lars' own story, remember that it is the life of one human being. A totally ordinary yet remarkable human being with an unusual, many-faceted life history to share with you. Enjoy it. You can be sure that only one thing is better: to be his friend and close to the well itself— just as clear and certain in his life and pen as during an earlier life. He has lived at least eight. Well met during your ninth, Lars.

Ulf Mårtensson

THANK YOU ALL…

This book is the result of a whole lot of help from a whole lot of people (many will be in the name index in the back of the book but far from all). I want and need to mention Pär Ståhlqvist, Britt Norrman, Sven Lundin, Staffan Lundberg and Ulf Mårtensson, who all contributed immensely to this book, each in his or her own way.

The true benefit of a long life is that it offers you the opportunity to see and experience more. If you have the slightest interest in how the world will be for your grandchildren, you do what you can to stay around. To be able to do that, it helps if you keep an active mind and are blessed with a healthy body.

A combination of those two factors has provided me with what I believe can be described as an extraordinary life that I invite you to share and challenge. Plus, I still feel that I have a few things undone.

Aside from the various events and occupations that have provided me with a never ceasing workload, there was this watershed in my life when at the age of fifty I moved to America. From having been somebody in my native Sweden, I became nobody in the U.S. Now I have thirty years on each continent. I was able thanks to America, to avoid the deadline for the working mind when at 65, Swedes are obligated to leave professional life to retire into some mental hibernation. Or as the retired railroad stationmaster said: "There goes a train. I don't give a damn. There goes another. I still don't give a damn."

Through my life I've met and befriended many, some became close while others passed through quickly. Lifelong friends such as Gösta Pryzelius, Joel Haskel, Åke Hjorth or Ingemar Essén, who covered every area, from stage to boardrooms are deeply rooted in my memory and heart. We were a colorful group of individualists tied together since childhood in a rarely seen friendship where quite possibly I was considered the most individual. I found I had a gift with the pen when my school year essays graded as high as my older friend Jan Olof Olsson (later JOLO, beloved columnist in Sweden's largest daily, *Dagens Nyheter*). I secured an income early on by supplying a local paper with news from school athletics at a penny per line. Barbro Alving, BANG in Dagens Nyheter, later gave me the key to writing: "Say what you have to say in the nut graph and allow them to cut freely from the back of your story."

I sailed through the regional newspapers for some time, rubbing elbows with giants such as Pekka Langer or Stig Gits Olsson in the beginning, prior to landing jobs at Times and BBC in London. Later, through adventures in Africa and as anchorman of the main Swedish news channel, growing my own communications conglomerate and land developer in the Bahamas I found myself in entirely new areas of work.

Friends and colleagues of the publishing patriarch Abbe Bonnier or Tore Nilsson are likely sitting somewhere, wondering "Ottoson, whatever did you look for in America?"

Good question. But, so far, so good.

Lars-Henrik Ottoson

LARS-HENRIK OTTOSON

THE BURDEN OF PAST GENERATIONS

If, as they say, it is true that you can trace your habits and character through the genes of your forefathers, then I am getting pretty close to understanding why and what has made me what I am. Many genes may sleep for generations before they are let loose on you. In my case it seems as if they were all in a huarry to get out and meet right away. I have tried to solve the puzzle presented by the characters of Counts and inn keepers, beer maidens, lumber jacks, sailors, railroaders, adventurers, tailors and royal servants, stage stars and emigrants.

My paternal great grandfather's name was Lars Ottoson. He was born in 1825. He had a farm, Råbyholm, in the southern Swedish province of Skåne and only a mile from the university city of Lund. He had three daughters. It was rumored that the oldest, Lisa, had been involved in an unhappy love affair, seduced by the son of Count Otto Tott of the nearby Skabersjö Castle. Some say it was maybe not so but the fact remains that someone paid for Lisa to move to Copenhagen where my father Elvin Henrik Ottoson was born in April of 1880. My grandmother never revealed the name of the father and lived most of her life with the shame of an unwed mother. After some years in Copenhagen she moved to Lund where she supported herself by sewing and taking in laundry. She spent every penny she could on Elvin's school material, but the aforementioned Tott family of Skabersjö paid the main expense, the fee at the rather exclusive Cathedral School, for some reason. One needn't wonder why he was teasingly called "the aristocrat" at school. My grandmother never looked at another man until she was over seventy when one day, during her daily walk in the Humlegården Park in Stockholm, she met an elderly gentleman. As a result she untied her hair and went to the hairdresser for the first time in her life. The two of them continued to meet in the park for their daily stroll together for many years. She lived with us until her death in 1942.

My maternal great grandfather descended from a 300-year line of innkeepers interspersed occasionally with soldiers, no one rising over the rank of sergeant. All married local women except my great grandfather who went to England to learn the tailoring trade and married a fisherman's daughter from Hull. Returning to Stockholm he made a good life by tailoring the King's uniforms. They had one child, Edward, who became the railroad stationmaster in the university city of Uppsala. He married Jane Malmlöf and fathered six children with a wide spread of interests and occupations.

If you believe in the effects of genes, you will find them working on the six children.

Uncle Helge went to sea when he was 13. He fought in the Spanish Civil War, became a lumberjack and then, in his old age built a rowing boat in his sitting room of his third floor apartment in the Stockholm suburb of Stadshagen. He launched it over the balcony to the delight of some and consternation of others who thought he was crazy. He had a two horsepower outboard engine and said he needed a boat to go with it.

My mother and father.

Aunt Swea was hardly twenty when she went to America on her own and married a German immigrant, Carl Zinnel, in Galveston, Texas.

Uncle Olle, known as Kungs-Olle, was the first chauffeur for the Swedish king, Gustav V. One rainy day, driving the king to his summer palace, Tullgarn, he drove off the road. To this day the place is called 'Kungens Kurva' (The King's Curve).

When he resigned, the King helped him financially to start the first cab company in Sweden.

Uncle Knut did not miss a working hour during more than forty years with Statens Järnvägar (The Government's Railroad – Amtrak). His knowledge of Swedish history was unsurpassed. Every Sunday during my pre-teen years he walked me through Gamla Stan (The Old City) and every Sunday gave me a new history lesson. We always ended up listening to the military band during the Changing of the Guards at the palace. Every Sunday as we walked from the palace he pointed to a second floor window in a building saying:

"And there my boy is where your great grandfather tailored His Majesty the King's uniforms. Knut never married but when he retired he met a lady who was also a railroad retiree. They even happened to live in the same building. Every other month or so, uncle Lnut changed his locks when he felt that he had "had enough of old ladies for a while."

Aunt Nickan married a shopkeeper. Together they opened a general store in the industrial community of Hallstavik. They were successful until the Konsum cooperative opened a large store. They moved to Stockholm and opened a tobacco shop on Fleminggatan.

My father Elvin Henrik began his professional life as a bank clerk. He was the leading solo tenor of the Academic Choir in Lund. When the choir was invited to perform at the opening of the new Concert House (Konserthuset) in Gothenburg, a Danish agent heard my father and within months he had leading roles in musicals in Copenhagen. The year was 1907. He returned to Sweden and soon starred at the Oskars Theater in Stockholm. It was said that female fans almost climbed over each other at the stage door every night. He liked it and made the best of it until he met my mother, Märta Kristina Olsson.

Märta was the youngest of the Olsson children. She had a beautiful voice and everyone encouraged her to audition when the Oscars Theater looked for a new young fresh female voice.
She was nervous and felt like an ugly duckling in her home made dress among the many more theater savvy girls looking for the same part.

She kept going back in the line when my father said "next!" Suddenly she was the only one on the stage. The orchestra started playing and she began singing, but after a minute she flopped. My father decided to help her because he had already discovered a beautiful coloratura soprano. He dismissed the orchestra, kept only the pianist, placed himself on a chair at the stage and said: "Now Märta you sing for me." And she sang herself right into his heart. He just got up from the chair, walked over and said,

"Märta I love you and I want to marry you."

He was 40. She was 22 and scared to death by his remark. In the evening mother Olsson, who could be a battle-axe, came to the theater to read him the law. However, he charmed her and three weeks later Elvin married Märta. They remained happily married until he died, much too young, in 1952 and he never looked at another woman. I was the only child.

LARS-HENRIK OTTOSON

STOCKHOLM IN THOSE DAYS

The Stockholm in which I came of age, late 1920s and 1930s, stretched from Valhallavägen in the north to Ringvägen in the south. There were barges delivering firewood docking by Strandvägen. There was a regiment in the midst of the city. People with a bit of money had live-in maids who were picked up by the kitchen door on Wednesday (piglördag) mostly by some soldier. For 15 öre (two pennies) you could spend the whole day on a city tram. There were namnanrop on (name calls) telephone.

Stockholm was a city with peaceful nights. The radio station closed at 10 pm. Here and there people still trickled from restaurants and theaters but by midnight the city was asleep. The streets lay empty except for some whores looking for customers around Stureplan and Birger Jarl's Street. And there was a secret nightclub, Grotta Azzurra, somewhere in town and known only to the people in the know.

The Stockholm that counted lived on Östermalm towards Odengatan. Those so to say bordering to be among the counted lived on Norrmalm or Vasastaden with a poor offspring in the north called Siberia. In the section called Kungsholmen there was of course the rather fashionable Norr Mälarstrand along the water's edge. The southern part of the city on the hills, Södermalm, you just did not talk about or visit. I think I was 12 years old before I set my foot there. It was rumored that people even lived in a suburb called Enskede. Outside of the city there were only three livable areas: Djursholm, Lidingö and Äppelviken. Stockholm's upper and middle classes were a rather snob infested bunch.

We were in a transition period from cabaret king Ernst Rolf to a more intellectual cabaret reign by Karl Gerhard at the Folkan theater at Östermalms torg (the square in the Östermalm area).

The last "punch veranda" disappeared when Hotel Anglais closed at Stureplan and Hasselbacken was converted to a restaurant school. Bellmansro on Djurgården burned down. A new generation of celebrities and business leaders favored the Riche and Cecil. The ABA airline president Calle Björkman was the city's party king, Anders de Wahl the great name at Dramaten (the Royal Theater in Stockholm) and Olof Winnerstrand the Sunday stroller, "flaneur" on Strandvägen. Sickan Carlsson was Sweden's Mary Pickford and Edvard Persson the most popular movie star.

Then WWII hit this somewhat idyllic country. The guy running a hot dog stand and being a member of Landstormen (sort of a national guard) suddenly found bossing drafted company presidents created a social equilibrium previously unthinkable. Food coupons were a pain in the neck but the farmers made more money than ever. Stockholm became the spy capital of Europe. The Russian, British, American and German embassies were on the same street. You found Italians and Germans dining at the table next to British embassy staff. My wife Lill worked as a CPA and used to enjoy talking to an American whose money she handled. He seemed irritated and nervous one day. He had just killed a German in a telephone booth on Strandvägen to prevent him from reporting him as a double agent. It was made into one of the greatest spy movies after the war starring, I believe, Charlton Heston.

It was also a time when the smell of wet wool combined with the smell of sweat from unwashed armpits filled trams and busses. The Swedes were a real dirty people at the time. The women were a bit better than the men who changed shirt and underwear only once a week and we did not shower more often either. Except my father who, after riding his horse for an hour, took a sauna bath every day at Sturebadet.

The city had into the 1940's just as many out-houses as flush thrones. Indoor bathrooms were a luxury. Dirty feet were standard in the soccer team's dressing rooms. When I took a girl home after a school dance and stood caressing her by the stairwell, I can still sense the smell of unwashed virginity. Most likely I did not smell much better to her in a suit that had gone a few years without dry cleaning.

Just as now, old people talked about the good old days. The only good about them was that they gave me a chance to experience an historical world period close up and experience the arrival of a modern era, although so much more peaceful as the problems moved further away in time.

One of Sweden's greatest writers, Lubbe Nordström, described what he called 'Lort-Sverige' (Filth-Sweden) as it really was. Farm workers lived in housing much like migrant workers in the U.S. today. Albert Engström's trashy "koling" and leather faced fishermen started to leave room for Åsa Nisse and pop idols like Snoddas, a bandy player, an athlete who surprised the radio audience by being able to sing a ditty. And all the time we heard the bassó voice of the comic Thor Modén's booming rumblings, "wonderful times, glorious times.." ('Strålande tider, härliga tider').

Surbrunnsgatan 66 in Stockholm.

CHILDHOOD AND THE EARLY YEARS

My life began in a house in Äppelviken and my first contact with the press was when as a three year old I was pictured on the front page of the magazine Vecko Journalen helping to hoist the flag. They were great years for Märta and Elvin Ottoson. They filled the entertainment parks during the summers and the Oskars Theater the rest of the year. Father bought a big open Dodge and used it as the first auto touring entertainers in Sweden performing at Folkparkerna - the entertainment parks created by the labor unions in practically every town in Sweden. It was quite a taxing job for my mother as she had to get out of the car to open the cow gates that straddle the roads everywhere, There was basically only one gate free road, the main one running north-south. My mother could tell you, for instance, that there were 48 cow gates between Kalmar and Jönköping.

The labor unions never forgot how two famous artists like Märta and Elvin took the trouble to perform where most artists wouldn't bother. They helped my parents through the perils of the depression. The car and the house went back to the bank after my father financed a lavish musical for a tour that happened during the worst rainy summer in over 50 years. As a folkpark had mostly outdoor seating my father had no choice but to cancel the tour. But he paid every artist, musician and technician for a full summer, because that was the way he was. And that's why we had to move into a smaller apartment on Grevgatan in Stockholm near Sandrew's grocery store.

In the building where we lived I noticed how a nice old lady went out at almost fixed hours twice a day. I made sure that I was there to open the gate for her as she always gave me five öre, which I used on cookie crumbs at Sandrews. I shared them with my pal Agne Eriksson as we built fortifications from magazine cut outs and then battled each others' tin soldiers with paper bullets.

The road back was long and hard for my father but he walked it with uncommon dignity. Even if he did not even have 15 öre for a tram fare, he still looked as if he could buy the town. His motto was: "Walk straight, keep your head up and pay your tailor."

While many artists from the golden pre depression age of musicals sat at home and waited for the phone to ring, the folkpark people around the country always saw to it that there was some work for Märta and Elvin. It was their way of recognizing my parents. Then, as the country worked itself out of the depression, came more work - radio programs, musicals and films. We moved to a bigger place on Odengatan.

My father had been able to rebuild his career although he had to leave the leading musical parts to younger artists. He left the lover parts to Lars Egge, who handed them to Per Grundén, who handed them to Jarl Kulle after whom the old style musical or operetta more or less died in Sweden.

My grandmother who had watched over me with loving care died in 1942. Her passing allowed us to move to a smaller and more convenient apartment. I even had a room with a private toilet, which made all my school friends come home to see it before they believed it. We also had our first refrigerator. Now we did not have to put the milk outside on the windowsill any more.

The main income still came from Folkpark concerts, radio programs and New Year's Eve performances. The cinemas in Stockholm all filled their New Year's Eve with live artist performances. My parents had a taxi outside to take them from one movie house after another. At midnight they led the count down at some theater. Then the audience just walked out into the New Year's night. Not much fuss. My parents made 75 kronor from each theater of which fifteen went to the piano player and ten to the driver. They could do four to six movie houses during the evening and that was a lot of money in those days - enough for my father to get a tartar sandwich and a schnapps at the Metropol restaurant around the corner and a bit later, a drink, a 'grogg' with the owner.

We now lived at Surbrunnsgatan on the fourth floor of a typical inner city apartment building. There was an asphalt court with two garbage dumpsters that were emptied once a week spreading some stench up the walls of the enclosed yard hitting the kitchen windows. There was the scaffold for beating carpets. When not used it served as a thing for us kids to climb. Twice a year we carried our carpets and area rugs down for beating. It was quite an effort just bringing them down from the fourth floor, as they did not fit in the elevator. There was a laundry room in the basement. Each apartment was allocated two days a month access to the laundry room. You had to be down there early to light and stoke the fire under the big laundry basin. We hung the laundry to dry up in the attic where there was a mangling machine to press - hand powered of course. Two more families lived on the floor and we shared cleaning the fourth floor stairs and lobby.

The rent was 400 kronor a month, which in those days was equivalent to about $80. Due to government rent regulations that did not allow any rent increases above living cost index, it did not allow the owners of the building much more than paying for keeping the elevator running. Today it would cost almost $300,000 on the black market to get even a rental contract to that apartment.

I attended the Norra Latin High School and those of you readers who are familiar with the Swedish language might enjoy the official name of the old school: Högre Allmänna Läroverket for Gossar å Norrmalm. I only devoted my interest at school to those subjects that interested me like Swedish language, history, geography, the high school literary club Concordia, the school dances and, of course, the soccer team. I spent many an hour when I should have been in class at the Cafe Mocca Efti together with similar mates, having coffee, smoking cigarettes and debating life. Some times instead of going to the cafe I went to the Central Station, bought a platform ticket and just sat there watching the trains, dreaming that I was on board traveling south. My relationships with my teachers were either very good or very bad. My French teacher greeted the class with "Good Morning my friends and Ottoson."

During summers my parents boarded me at a farm in Skåne, Karindal, by the village of Spannarp near the city of Ängelholm. They paid, I think, about 75 kronor a month. They were wonderful summers, but at the same time they displayed a world just as romantically false as a painting by Carl Larsson. The flag flying over the big house. The coffee table set on the lawn. Old Blenda from the kitchen feeding the geese. The children of the farm hands jumping in the haystacks or taking the horses to the stable. As far as anyone could see and judge, everything was the way it was supposed to be out in the country. That was unless you came too close to it. Still those summers stay in my memory as the happiest in my life.

Vera Hagander, a truly merry widow, owned Karindal in the 1930's. She leased the farming to two brothers Persson. She had two sons, Ulf and Hugo. The latter became one of the entertainer Povel Ramel's favored partners called Loppan Hagander. When Vera, who also was Swedish tennis doubles champion a couple of years, took her Model A-Ford to a Saturday dance at the Ängelholm Stadshotell or the beach restaurant at Skälderviken, the local bachelors drowned in waves of desire.

"Is Misses going out now again?" sort of stated Blenda, who was paid ten kronor a month and had saved enough when the farm was sold to open a luncheonette in the village of Klippan.

Sundays we boys were allowed to go with Vera to the beach at Skälderviken. I remember how the farmhand kids used to wave at us when we drove by. Their "seaside resort" was one of the marl pits. There they sailed their home made bark boats. Now and then someone fell in and drowned in the muddy water.

The farmhand row of houses was far enough from the main house not to be "disturbing" in any way. When the men came home from work they washed at the pump where the families got their water. That's when the women left for the fields to milk the cows.

One reason for me being welcome at the farmhand row was that I had a soccer ball. The farm hand kids were never allowed to play with the two soccer balls that Gustav Persson kept for the local soccer team, IK Salamis. Gustav was the leading farm hand at Karindal and the best soccer player. I thought positively in my admiration that he qualified for the national team. His brother Knut was almost as good. IK Salamis played in division V and the matches on the sports area behind the railroad station were always timed when there was enough time between trains for the stationmaster to be the referee. I remember how Gustav sat on the porch putting plugs in the team's soccer boots and watching us kids as we fought for the ball. He would look up and say, "Hondans, you damned kids play soccer and don't you damn fight." Football cleats were expensive and Salamis only had eleven pairs for its eleven players. So when training they had to use their wooden clogs tied to their feet. Eight of the team's eleven players came from Karindal. Whenever they won a match there was a coffee gala at the row. And there were these mysterious male visits to behind the big wood stack. As if the women did not know that the men sneaked back there for a snifter of aquavit.

Those bony farm hands were still a long way from organized labor like their brethren up north. Skåne was still a feudal area with big estates and castles that resisted anything that smelled of unionized farm labor.

Midsummer came with the big democratic gathering at Karindal. At the long table by the midsummer pole, the farm workers and their families were treated to a feast of coffee, cakes and a snifter or two for the men.
"Welcome Karlsson."
"Thank you missus."
"Glad to see Amanda."
"Thank you missus."
She always used the last name for the men and the first name for the women. At the end of the table sat the guests from the city that had come to experience a real midsummer out in the country. The People drank from the plate with a piece of sugar in the mouth. The sound of slurping traveled along the table. Vera Hagander threw out remarks to lighten the event. "Don't care about that Amanda, just let the boy have as many cookies as he wants. Won't Karlsson have another glass? Just

drink up and have a good time Andersson." Finally the accordion player arrived and the dancing could start. Skåne farms and estates were like the great green lawn where the geese walked. Beautiful to look at but full of goose dump.

Skabersjö.

LARS-HENRIK OTTOSON

THE REALITIES OF GROWING UP

The reality of life suddenly caught up with me in the summer of 1936 during a visit to relatives in Hamburg, Germany. It hit me at the Radhaus Platz, the main square at Hamburg City Hall, among thousands listening to Adolf Hitler speaking. I was packed in and needed to go to the bathroom. Of course there wasn't any in sight. However, I spied a tree some 50 meters away and figured that if I could make it there I might be able to press against the tree and pee unnoticed. As I was finally relieving myself a young Hitler Jugend behind me hit me as he threw out his arm shouting Heil Hitler. My pee stream changed direction. It ran down the boots of an SA officer. He called an SA guard and had me taken to an SS officer in the City Hall basement. Now an SS officer was a darn size worse than an SA officer. I figured at least execution.

I soon found that he was mad not so much for my having pissed on the boots of an SA officer - about that he couldn't care less. But he was madder than hell that I had had the audacity to take a leak while Adolf Hitler was speaking. I was saved by the fact that my relative was General von Schaumburg, a top Luftwaffe officer. Speaking to him by telephone, the SS officer sat up straight in the chair as if at attention.

"Of course Herr General, but it's hard to believe that this young man is only fourteen."

My long pants had deceived him. German boys my age wore shorts. The SS officer sent me home with an escort. Hitler was still orating.

After a week I moved to another relative on Rothenbaumchausse near the Alster Lake. I often walked over to Uhlenholster Fährhaus hoping to save enough of my weekly allowance to rent one of the canoes and paddle on the Alster. I was in luck one day when a girl sitting in a canoe said, " Do you want to paddle? This is a two-seater and I might need some help." If I wanted to paddle?!! Cruising up and down the Alster and through the canals leading to the harbor she asked if I would like a beer. I had never had a beer, but I felt it would disappoint her if I said no. She had a whole basket of beers and I was wondering how her parents could allow her to drink when she asked if I was hungry.

"No," she said, "I don't have any food with me but we can go to my home and get something to eat."

I wondered what her parents would say when she came home with a boy. But there were no parents in the apartment behind the Hotel Vier Jahreszeiten. She lived alone! While she went into the kitchen I looked around. At a desk I found her passport. My God, she was 34 years old. She was as old as my mother!!

I silently eased myself towards the door, opened it quietly and ran. My God did I run!! Until, that is, I felt the urge to visit a restroom. I saw this cut off of a narrow lane looking like the entrance to a public urinal the way they looked in Stockholm. So I walked into what actually was a long narrow street lined with windows in which half naked women exposed themselves to lure customers.

'Geh Mal nach Hause mit deinem fünfzehn Jahre'

(Take all of your fifteen years and go home), someone yelled at me.

My long pants did not fool these ladies. For reasons I cannot explain, I did not turn around to leave. I just walked the block long whore stroll – but right in the middle, looking straight ahead.

Half naked women were per se nothing new to me. When I visited my parents backstage at theaters there were always dancers in various stages of dress or undress and ballet girls changing. But of course these girls by Gänzemarkt did not exactly look like ballerinas.

After that summer my parents said:

"He isn't the same boy since he came home from Hamburg."

A FRUGAL MOVIE KING

When we moved from the suburban house to the apartment on Grevgatan, Anders Sandrew spent a lot of time behind the counter of his grocery store. He would sell five öres worth (a penny) of yeast while he used the shop phone to get the day's ticket sales at one of his cinemas. It was said that he had a brother who made some money on the black market during the First World War and used it to open this store. No one ever saw or heard of any brother after that.

Many years later when a movie ticket cost 1.35 kronor (less than $2) I sat in his frugal office above the store. He himself never moved into the lavish offices above the Palladium cinema on Kungsgatan where he housed his producers, directors and creative staff. His personal assistant, who no one ever knew except as Andersson, came in and told him that a Mrs. Lindgren had called and complained that she had bought a ticket at the Astoria cinema on Nybrogatan but could not see the film properly because of a column. Sandrew stroked his nose, as he used to do when he was deep in thought, and said: "I see, Mrs. Lindgren could not see the film properly. Then send her the 1.35 for the ticket but deduct for the postage."

Many were the prominent people who found that when Anders Sandrew invited them for lunch it mostly consisted of toast or cereal and a cup of coffee in the office above the grocery store.

Anders Sandrew was generous with himself but frugal when it came to money. After buying his first cinema, Astoria, he kept buying more, saying that if an item sells it's like in the grocery store; you buy more of it. Yeast or movie house - the same rule. Within ten years he had the largest chain of cinemas in the country, the largest production company, and leading studios. But he himself never moved out of his office above the store on Grevgatan.

My friend, the cabaret star Git Gay, told me that once after a very successful cabaret opening a big bunch of red roses was delivered to her apartment. She couldn't believe it until a couple of hours later when someone from Mr. Sandrew's office knocked on her door asking to see the roses to count them against the bill.

The greatness of Anders Sandrew showed in the simplicity with which he solved big problems and his common sense. He did not demand loyalty. He just received it. He knew everyone who worked for him, the name of their spouses and children and he regularly asked about their well-being. It meant a lot to a lady who managed the ticket booth in a cinema in Sundsvall to get a phone call from Sandrew inquiring about ticket sales and at the same time being asked how little Karl was doing at school.

Loyalty is what kept world-renowned cinematographer Sven Nykvist working for him until Sandrew died. He stayed for 25,000 kronor a year when he could have gotten ten times the amount in the USA or England.

"He was the one that told his directors to give me a chance or get out," said Sven who catapulted to world fame with Ingmar Bergman and Woody Allen. "That's why I am staying."

Of course many writers and directors felt frustrated when they some times had to wait for his housekeeper to read a script before he approved it. He explained it to me once after asking how the fine old lady, my grandmother Lisa, was. I did not tell him that my grand mother died many years before. But he remembered her. I wrote some material for his cabarets and he explained it to me.

"You see," he said and stroke his nose, "Ellen is just a simple Swedish woman and if she likes a script then eighty percent of Swedes will like it and see the film. But if she does not like the script people won't see the movie."

Of course now and then he gave in to great movies like Barrabas with Sven Nykvist at the camera. Seeing the movie after it was done, Sandrews stroke his nose saying, 'well, I guess we have lost a million now." In the sound studio one day with the musical academy professor Hilding Rosenberg, Sven Nykvist introduced the professor to Anders Sandrew who stroke his nose and said: "Professor Rosenberg creating the music to this film, I think that sounds terrible." He was, as usual, blunt but right. The music was bad.

Anders Sandrew never entered the light he created for others. His big car remained in the garage while he used his bicycle. Now and then he surfaced at one of his cinemas in Stockholm. If he saw dirt on the floor and staff busy he took a broom and swept the floor himself.

I saw big openings at any one of his theaters, like Oskars, with a full range of a tuxedo crowd. When the show started Sandrew came in with a chair and sat down in the back by the door and was gone just as unnoticed afterwards.

Anders Sandrew visited London in 1947 to negotiate a deal with the Rank organization. To announce his arrival he sent the following telegram to Rank, which undoubtedly raised some eyebrows: "I am a coming man." At the Savoy Hotel in London the staff expected some handouts upon his departure, the way it always worked with celebrities. The room staff stood lined up as Sandrew walked from one to the other, pressed half-a crown in their hands and said, "thank you very much, thank you very much."

Was he a penny pincher? Undoubtedly. But it was in a manner that gave you the impression that he was not mean but that he did not know any other way. He was what we in Swedish would call a real luring. When we two had dinner at a pub one night and ordered a pitcher of beer but only drank half of it, Sandrew told me not to pay for more than half the beer.

SCHOOL YEARS AND ON

From my room on the fourth floor at Surbrunnsgatan, I could look out over the Hamburger brewery and the brewery horses very similar to those featured by Budweiser in America today. I had two years of high school left before matriculating with the right to wear the white cap. I had an allowance of three crowns a week which just covered the expenses of a school dance evening or a visit to the outdoor dance floor at Skansen and Bob Larnys famous orchestra.

My first love lasted one night. Her name was Ragna Nyblom and I had had my eyes on her for a month but never dared to approach her - partly because she was mega popular and partly because I really could not dance. Those were two good reasons for admiring her at a distance. I certainly was not a shy guy; I just did not want to embarrass myself in front of people.

It was fifteen minutes past nine, May 27 when I found myself in a crowd surrounding Ragna. She caught sight of me, put her arm around my waist and said that I was allowed to buy her a cup of coffee. I thought heaven had come to Skansen and I already had advanced plans for further progress. Bob Larny's orchestra played Blue Skies, her favorite melody. They should not have done that because now she wanted us to dance! After some minutes on the dance floor she said, " Aren't you going to turn around soon?" She disappeared among her friends. As crushed and unhappy as only a teenager can be, I wandered alone along the waters of Strandvägen.

The next day I tried to work off my shame and frustrations playing table tennis with a frenzy for a quarter stake per set at the table tennis courts below the Carlton Hotel at Kungsgatan.

At school I concentrated my efforts on the Literary Club but took it easy through the classes. I had to do some classes twice so ended up with more school buddies than most.

Perhaps you remember the movie Frenzy ('Hets') with Alf Kjellin as a schoolboy tormented by a teacher, Caligula (played by actor Stig Järrel). I experienced "my Caligula" in the form of my French teacher Gösta Franke. He was the one who began lessons by saying, "Good morning my friends - and Ottoson." The reason for his aversion could be traced to his habit to walk around and slam the desktops. One day he saw an issue of the magazine La Vie Parisien in my desk.

"So Ottoson is a student of French literature I can see," he said. The magazine was the closest you could get to pornography in those days, but lame in comparison to today's Playboy. I could not very well say that I had rented it for the day for ten öre from my buddy Ingemar Essén. We all rented from Ingemar, a future bank director. Teacher Franke said that as I apparently already was familiar with the French pictures he would relieve me of any efforts to learn the language and that he could guarantee me a D. And so it went for weeks until one day when Franke posted a question that no one knew the answer to. But I did. So I raised my hand, Franke walked around me a couple of times and then he asked the class, "My friends shall we dare to hear what Ottoson has to say?" All nodded. When I answered correctly, Franke hurried back to his podium, climbed up on a chair, raised his arms and said, " My God, Ottoson answered correctly, Hallelujah." Thereafter, in addition to his usual greeting excepting me, he now added, " My friends, what happened on February 12?" In unison the class answered, "Ottoson answered a question correctly."

I fully understand that Ingemar Essén ended up in the financial world. He had a flair for making money. At a time when my weekly allowance was three kronor, Ingemar always kept a ten kronor bill in his wallet as a reserve. We called him Buttjo because he was a pretty big guy and a terrific swimmer. School champion. After swimming the length of an Olympic size pool, the sports paper Idrottsbladet headline read: BUTTJO BEATS THE SEALS OF THE ZOO.

At home his divorced mother called him 'gullungen' (cutie pie). Their apartment at Odengatan was the place where we gathered to play the latest records and do a bit of petting when the mother wasn't around. I can't remember if I went there for the records, the girls or mother Essén's cakes. It was probably a combination of all three. Years later, when we all so to say had arrived, I met Ingemar guiding some prominent businessmen around. I slapped him on the back and said, " Hi Gullungen." He turned red from embarrassment so I quickly asked how he was doing and he gave me a classic answer, " Oh you know old friend, the desk grows with the responsibility."

The youth of Stockholm in those days were either 'Swingpjattar' or 'Nalensnajdare'. The former were mainly high school kids, who wore long hair and wide brimmed hats. The latter were working class youth who cut their hair short and wore hats with narrow brims. Skansen's dance rotunda and school dances ruled Swingpjatten's Saturdays. Nalensnajdaren danced at Nalen (hence the name) a dance palace in central Stockholm. We used to say that the difference was that Swingpjatten's family had a modern AGA range in the kitchen while Nalensnajdaren's family most likely still used a wood stove. When the club, Concordia, that I chaired at school, decided to have a debate about the two factions, the auditorium was filled to over capacity. Reps of both sides were well prepared. All the daily papers were there and one headlined the event: *The most remarkable event in Stockholm since the palace fire in 1897 took place yesterday at the Norra Latin high school.*

It was September 17, 1941 and the protocol after the debate read:

> *Anyone who happened to be near the Norra Latin this Saturday must have seen that something extraordinary was going on. There was a crowd filing in through the iron gates filling the auditorium. There were people everywhere. Over 1,300 youngsters took up every inch, from floors to windowsills. The chairman, Lars Henrik Ottoson greeted everyone welcome with a short and hard-hitting speech opening a debate that will long be remembered.*

Norra Latin was the city's most prominent soccer school. John Anderberg who was center forward in AIK,

Stockholm's leading first division team, did not qualify for the school team. They said he was too cautious, afraid of hurting his expensive legs in rough school football. From the team that won the school championship three players went on to represent Sweden, one became head of the Swedish Soccer Association and one coached the nationals.

It was here that my journalistic career began. *Svenska Dagbladet* paid me ten öre (about 2¢) per line to report about school sporting events. From these rather insignificant events I was promoted to report on club events and fringe sports for 15 öre per line. I soon learned to create long sentences that were difficult to cut. I also soon had a network of club officials who called me reporting on events.

Concordia somewhat helped me cope with my French teacher Franke whose hatred I traced to my father. Franke, who was a violinist, had auditioned for my father for a position with the Oskars Theater Orchestra. My father, being a director and producer, had turned him down.

Its literary and theater circles lessened the pain in the neck of going to school where, by the way, I had some respect from, in my mind, more intellectual teachers. I made a radio version of August Strindberg's Gustaf Vasa and wired it to all the classrooms from a studio in the music room. I understand that my Swedish teacher put in some good words about me among his colleagues. When I asked him why, in my literary pieces I could not, according to him, start a sentence with the word 'och' (and), he answered, "Because Ottoson is not yet a Strindberg."

My ability as a school actor was inferior to that of Gösta Pryzelius and Erland Josephsson, and Ingemar Pallin all of whom reached prominence as actors. Pryzelius spent 35 years with Dramaten in Stockholm and ended his career as star of a TV series called Rederiet – the

Shipping Line. When he died a few years ago the headline in a daily paper read: "He was not God, but close to it." Erland Josephsson became one of Ingmar Bergman's most favored actors (Scenes from a Marriage) and later succeeded Bergman as head of Dramaten. Ingemar Pallin became the first Swedish actor to play Hamlet at Elsinore Castle (Helsingør, Denmark).

Gösta Pryzelius and I became life long friends from the days we dated together. His last act in life was a half finished letter to me on his lap. We were both Latin students so when we created an entertainment duo for the school dances we called ourselves Ego and Company. As part of the entertainment we engaged a newly formed band that debuted as Povel Ramel and His Buller Dogs (Noise dogs). I remember that already during that first season Povel played one of his greatest hits: Johansson's Boogie Woogie Waltz. Povel went on to become the number one entertainer, musical creator, and cabaret launcher in Sweden for many years to come.

Gösta had bigger ambitions however, than cabaret spoofs. For school-play our last year in school he wanted us to perform *The Merchant of Venice*, which would allow him to play Shylock. Erland, Ingemar and I thought it was a tad overly ambitious, but Gösta was pushing it hard. As we wrestled with the problem of who could possibly be the director, Gösta suddenly had an idea. "Listen," he said, "there is a guy who runs an amateur stage in the Old City, Gamla Stan, and I think he can do it." A few days later Gösta reported that this guy who was the son of a pastor in Gamla Stan would do it for 250 kronor ($30). His name was Ingmar Bergman.

At the gate to our school, Olle, the gatekeeper, looked at Ingmar Bergman and said "And who might you be and whom do you want to see?" For forty years that meeting became Gate Olle's most favorite story, quoting Bergman as saying, "I am the director Ingmar Bergman!"

I have never forgotten that first Bergman entrance into the school's auditorium. Wearing a beret, smoking a cigar, probably to disguise that he was not much older than any of us, he ordered a table and a chair, sat down and looked at us and a couple of girls that we had "borrowed" from the girls' school at Sveaplan. He did not say anything for a couple of minutes - just looked at us as if some dog had let us in. He was very impressive and we thought he must be a great director. He started off by rearranging the script moving part of the performance from the stage to the aisles and the balcony. We started to regard him as a genius. To this day Erland Josephsson says, "Lars Henrik gave me a small part but Ingmar Bergman knew better." Erland finally played the judge, Gösta played Shylock of course and I played Don Bassanio. I cannot remember Pallin's part but he was there with all his young energy.

After about a week I was called to the dean's office ('rektorsexpeditionen') and told that a couple of parents had called saying that their daughters had complained about Bergman using foul language.

"If Mr. Bergman does not clean up his mouth, I will not allow the play," said the dean, the 'rektor'.

Gösta, Erland and I had a meeting. We already understood that you don't tell Ingmar Bergman anything. Our solution was to change the girls for some that were more liberal. And so we did. We also decided to lock the doors during rehearsals.

The performance was - and probably still is - the best that has ever been staged in a high school. Dagens Nyheter, the largest newspaper in Sweden, gave the performance three full columns, which was more than for a premiere at the Royal Opera the same day.

It was Ingmar Bergman's first press and first meeting with two of the actors who came to be with him for over thirty years; Erland Josephsson and Gösta Pryzelius. A bit of stage history too, that both Ingmar and Erland later headed the Royal Dramatic Theater.

Allow me to quote the Concordia school protocol of November 30, 1940 covering the performance.

> *Then finally, everything was ready for that memorable day. After months of rehearsals and preparations under the Director Ingmar Bergman who had inspired Concordia's young actors with frenetic energy throwing the powerful lines of Shakespeare at each other.*
>
> *As the curtain, borrowed from Dramaten, rose to the mighty tunes of Marcia Carolus Rex, there was not a seat left in the auditorium. And what a sensational event it turned out to be as the director Bergman had inspired his young actors to remarkable performances and worked the lighting to effects that reminded one of another world. Among the actors you noticed foremost Gösta Pryzelius and Erland Josephsson as Antonio and Lars Henrik Ottoson as Bassanio. Svenska Dagbladet wrote that the performance went far above what could be expected and that the applause went wild as a sea of flowers surrounded the actors.*

This was the first time Ingmar Bergman's name was mentioned in the press, the first time his work caught the eyes of the critics and his first work before a huge audience as big as any he came to have at Dramaten.

I had shortly afterwards a brutal intermission in life. My father told me that if I did not make it to the top class I would have to enlist in the army. I did not make it, in my mind because of all my side interests, so Father shipped me off to the Svea Artillery Regiment. I had to do military service, as an enlisted soldier. There were only 70 of us at the regiment. The drafted soldiers called us rabbits. I don't think there was anyone less suited for military life than I was. What I did not know was that my father had conspired with two military friends to help teach me a lesson. One headed my regiment. Apparently he had also instructed my battery commander Captain

Bergman not to give me any slack. The Swedish army had at the time not changed much over the last hundred years. Our rifles were as our artillery from the previous century.

The group to which I belonged was supposed to eventually supply the army with non commissioned officers. However, that was a distant goal. After a year you might reach the level of vice corporal. I made the best out of my situation, as I fully understood that I had placed myself there. I liked the weapons training and getting my own horse to ride. Artillery was mounted and horse drawn. What I did not like were the hay filled mattresses full of critter and nightly stable watch which was supposed to be shared with three of the drafted soldiers who constantly beat you up to take their watch. They hated us and called us rabbits because we were being trained as their future tormentors.

The commanding officer of Battery 6, that I belonged to, looked like the old Swedish warrior King Karl XII and strutted like Mussolini. He seemed to like the simple farmers' lads but certainly not that totally different Ottoson.

He assigned me to take special care of his horse at the end of the day when the others went for food, and also on Sundays, when I was expected to feed and exercise the critter. He looked at his Battery crews as "material". He did not like me much because I was different. In the training rink I started by falling off the bareback critter all the time. Finally the equestrian teacher, Captain Wille Grut, Olympic decathlon gold medalist, got sick and tired of me and shouted,

"Damn you number twenty-three, tie your %^@! legs under the %^@! horse."

After three hours I was bleeding through my riding pants and it hurt. A corporal told me to put some caustic soap on it and of course you do as a superior tells you. He left the washroom laughing as I cried out. But you know, it helped to toughen my behind. Captain Bergman liked me even less than Captain Grut - mostly because I did not fit into the mold. Anyway, his horse seemed to like me as I took such good care of it and I think that made the captain even angrier.

Every Saturday morning we stood in line in the corridor as Captain Bergman went from one to the other and handed out weekend passes. When he reached me, he stopped, looked me in the eyes while he tore up my pass application and let the pieces fall to the floor. I did not pick them up and that annoyed him even more. I can still hear him say, "Either twenty-three is here because twenty-three is dumb as hell or twenty-three has been sent here to learn to shape up. Now I don't think that twenty-three is an idiot so I gather that twenty-three is here to learn to shape up. And goddamn, shape up you will..."

The caustic soda for my behind taught me that the lower the ranks the more they want to get back at you for what they themselves had to suffer. But officers..?
One day I found myself inhabited by small black insects in the most delicate place. I knew about head lice but these between my legs I did not recognize. So I went to the dispensary. A cigar-smoking doctor with the rank of major asked me if I knew what it was. Of course I did not.

"This, soldier, is the little Swedish household animal called bug. Where does twenty-three think he has caught them?"

"At a latrine sir!"

"Very well twenty-three, next time twenty-three meets that latrine, bring her with you when you come to see me."

As time passed I learned to ride good enough to participate in parades and to stay armed with a pitchfork when sharing a nightly stable watch with the regulars.

One night when I had stable watch my mother turned up outside the fence a bit away. She had bribed a guard at the gate to tell her how to find me. When she saw me she cried. The military uniform sizes were normalized for soldiers up to 6 feet max. I was 6'4 and looked like a scarecrow.

When the Finnish-Russian winter war started in 1939, the Swedish military woke up from decenniums of slumber in the arms of an officers' corps recruited from idle sons of noble families. I remember a drawing by Albert Engström picturing two lieutenants from the Blue Hussars watching a coral of horses. One pointed to a horse saying, " There is damn well my horse. Where is damn well your horse?"

Yes, Sweden woke up. We got new equipment, new uniforms and a new awareness of the world. Now I looked proper enough, enjoyed a new commanding officer and could date Britt Larsson, who lived on fashionable Strandvägen. I don't know why she took to me because my uniform was not that impressive. Her mother liked me less when I walked across the expensive Chinese carpet with my heavy military boots. Britt and I loved each other for a while but I had to pick her up from the kitchen entrance unseen by the mother. Britt, I found out later, married the owner of the famous Kramer Hotel in Malmö.

Svea Artillery Regiment was bordering the city. The tram swept by outside the gates. Christmas Eve I had guard duty. I stood there in the snow and cold watching the apartment lights and Christmas trees in the windows across the street. Christmas Day I had stable duty.

A couple of days later the regiment was to parade for the new chief and our battery was to parade in newly issued gas masks. The band was playing and we marched. I was left end wingman. My problem was that my mask fogged up. The column turned right. I kept going straight ahead and walked right into the band!

My sergeant was to issue my penalty. It consisted of being showered in my uniform and forced to sleep in it, two weeks of stable duty and one month without leave. I ended up at Garnisonssjukhuset, the military hospital on Kungsholmen with double pneumonia. My father and his friends felt I had had enough and pulled me back to civilian life to graduate at school.

Twenty years later - can you believe it - I was back at the regiment, which now had been converted to studios and offices for Swedish Television. Where I had slept I now had my desk. The rotunda where I learned to ride was now the studio from which I read the news and became known as 'Mr. Aktuellt' (named after 'Aktuellt,' the first regular evening news broadcast in Sweden). Of course there had passed a lot of water under the bridges by then.

"Did you get enough of the Nazis?" asked my dear Jewish friend Joel Haskel when I returned to school alluding to the fact that the Swedish officers corps was very "nazified". We came to share many a table tennis match after school and later in life he became the godfather of my children.

Even at school there were boys wearing brown shirts and the swastika. As embarrassing as it is to remember, there's no use denying it. The country had two Nazi parties. One led by a veterinarian from Molkom in Värmland, Birger Furugård, and one faster growing by Sven Olov Lindholm who was riding high on Nordic mythology and Viking Spirit. Joel found, just as I had, that it was good for the Nazis to be split between two parties because united they might have seriously infested the Swedish Parliament, the 'Riksdag'.

What attracted the schoolboys and pulled them to the youth movement during the 1930's were the uniforms and talk about the Nordic inheritance - Odin, Thor and

Valhalla. The troops and groups named themselves after their Viking heroes. My friend Joel Haskel was the best handball goalie in town. Still, in the dressing room he always sat by himself because he was, after all, a Jew!

One of Birger Furugård's leaders was a Captain John Åstrand who did not make major until he retired. He was an educated, intelligent man who was suspected for his German sympathies and who kept a signed photo of Adolf Hitler in his office. It always surprised my father how a man like John Åstrand could not see through the theatricals of the Nazi movement.

It was a time when Sweden had two strong voices against Hitler and his pack. One was Torgny Segerstedt, the editor of the leading newspaper in Gothenburg. His pen kept up a vitriolic chase of Nazism from the very day Hitler came to power. The other was Karl Gerhard, the Swedish cabaret king. His most famous song was "Den okända hästen från Troja." (The infamous horse from Troy.) So strong and loud were the voices of these two men that the Swedish government on a couple of occasions asked them to lower their voices as they hurt Swedish-German relationships. The only result of it of course, was that they raised their voices even louder. When the German Embassy hired its brown shirted Swedish lackeys to demonstrate outside the cabaret theater at Östermalmstorg, Karl Gerhard answered with piping out his Troy song over the square.

Actors of Norra Latin School in the green room getting ready for the first act of The Merchant of Venice *in 1940. Lars Henrik seated in front of the mirror between two girls. Photo courtesy of the Norra Latin School, Stockholm.*

LARS-HENRIK OTTOSON

IT CAN HAPPEN... AND IT DID

I walked around the block a couple of times - up along the brewery, Norrtullsgatan to the hospital and Frejgatan back to Surbrunnsgatan 60. It was snowing and cold. But I did not feel the cold. I felt nothing but despair and fear. For a while I stood looking towards the fourth floor bedroom window from the steps of the tobacco shop. I hoped to see the lights turned off so I could sneak in.

Lill was 19. I was 18. She was pregnant.

It would never have happened if we had not taken the same tram in the morning, she heading for office work and I heading for school. She got sort of curious about this guy who seemed to do his homework on the tram. I glanced at her and thought she was a looker. We met a Saturday several months later at a school dance. She caught me when they played the ladies turn. What happened then just happened. The teenage libido was just as strong in those days as today - the opportunities were, however, not as frequent.

I went to a phone booth and called Lill.

"Have you told your mother?"

"Yes, and you better come here and talk with her."

Elna Andersson was a formidable woman who sold veg-

etables at the market and did not fancy up her words.
"So, how is Lars going to take care of this?" she asked.
"I don't know."
"Now, he'd better know fast because tomorrow I am going to have a talk with Lars' parents!"

I went back to staring at the bedroom window. Maybe it was not such a good idea to wait for the lights to be turned off. Maybe telling mother when she was in bed was better than having her up.

I told her sort of abruptly and she sat straight up in the bed. She shook my father awake and told him almost hysterically.

He never liked to be awakened. He looked at her, patted her and said,
"There is very little we can do about it at this hour. Let's talk about it in the morning." And so he went back to sleep.

In the morning my mother was in the kitchen making coffee and talking to herself and decided to vent her frustration on her best friend Maja Persson who was married to a 'järnhandlare' (hardware store) in Hedemora.

I did not sleep much - if I slept at all. I only waited for my father to consider the situation after shaving and dressing.

I stood in the corridor outside the bathroom and waited. He seemed to shave unusually long this morning. My mother cried and mumbled. Then finally father exited the bathroom. He picked a shirt from a hanger. "Jaha," he said, and buttoned one button. The "Jaha" once again and then another button. There were five buttons on the shirt and he had to do them all before saying anything. He wasn't an actor for nothing.

He looked at me and said, "There is no excuse for what you did. Your future studies are now up in the air. I am sure you know how disappointed mother and I am."

"To say the least," said mother. " How could you, how could you?"

"I don't know," I answered. But of course I knew. I was just randy.

"What kind of girl is that?" said my mother.

My father looked at me. " I'll bet her mother right now says what kind of a boy is that?"

My father grew up with an unwed mother so he had some understanding about the subject. He felt, I think, more for Lill than for me. And rightly so: I was the first and the only man for her in a 33-year marriage. Our marriage found great strength through two very special people - my father and Lill's mother. Without the strong support of those two I don't think our marriage would have lasted past the first year.

Those were the days when you married the girl...at least if you had some decency.

As Lill continued her job, once again my father's good will among the trade unions paid off. The printer's union helped me to find a job as a junior sports writer at the daily *Arbetet* in Malmö. The pay was negligible. My father said he would pay for my room for three months. Then I would be on my own.

Chief editor Allan Vought, a Social Democratic primus, headed Sweden's best political daily. Work began at five in the morning. I was not used to those hours and at about eleven I would sneak into the room of the political Editor Johan Nilsson who, as a Member of Parliament, spent most of his time in Stockholm. I would just crawl under his desk and sleep for a while.

To this day what I remember most from the time at Arbetet are the fresh French rolls and the coffee from the bakery around the corner. For years, whenever I visited Malmö, I would go to the paper at five for coffee and a newly baked buttered "fralla" (French roll). It was also to see one of my idols, the sports editor Lennart

Strandberg. Once as a sprinter, he held the world record of 10.3 seconds for the 100-meter dash. At the Olympics in Berlin in 1936, he shared that record with the American Jesse Owens. They were supposed to fight it out in Berlin. After 50 meters they were shoulder to shoulder. After 55 meters Strandberg pulled a tendon in his right leg. I have seen those film frames many a time because whenever TV is closing in on the 100-meter event during an Olympics, they show this historical footage. Of course it also has something to do with Jesse Owens demonstrational rebuke of Hitler.

I have asked myself how good compared to today's sprinters was an athlete like Lennart Strandberg? And not only Strandberg but also many other athletes of his generation. Strandberg ran the 100 dashes in 10.3 seconds - in heavy shoes with long spikes and on soft charcoal breeze. He would have made 10 seconds today. Also think of the soccer players running and performing for 2 x 45 minutes in shoes that weighed more than a pound per piece. How would an equilibristic player like Nacka Skoglund have done in air light sneakers of today?

After three months, I secured a job with the Stockholm evening paper *Nya Dagligt Allehanda* as sports reporter. My boss was another Swedish sports legend, Håkan Lidman, one of the fastest 110-meter hurdlers in the world. My journalistic career started there. At Arbetet I had to spend half the time proofreading and running errands for the editors. The head of the reporter group told me once when I was laboring with some article, "if you can't write it in twenty minutes, don't write it.

At Allehanda I was assigned the sports that the older staff did not care about - handball, table tennis, tennis and boxing. Knowledge of the latter would come in handy almost twenty years later.

I wondered from the start about the fact that the Social Democratic press fared so poorly in Sweden when the party dominated the electorate. The Social Democrats for some reason did not read their own papers but read those of the opposition. Lennart Strandberg explained it in a way. What do you expect when you have had a great sports Sunday and have to cut out a whole page of the sports section to make room for neighborhood political reports? One after the other, I saw the SD papers die. I only have to think of my father in law, a union man. He subscribed to the rather right wing *Dagens Nyheter* while at the same time telling me that it is the duty of every Swede to vote for the Social Democrats.

At NDA I shared a desk with a table tennis champ and legendary radio commentator. I also worked under the legendary sports editor and international soccer referee R:et Eklöf. I remember how I felt about having "arrived" when I sat with him at a soccer game although my job was just to call in the results to the papers afternoon sports edition. Before Håkan Lidman came to head the sports pages while R:et prepared himself for a bigger position at Dagens Nyheter, a man called Gert Engström turned up from Harnäs where he apparently had headed the local office for *Gefle Dagblad*. He brought his bandy clubs and right away came up with the idea for a girlies spread in the Sunday sports edition. He suddenly found himself dating chorus girls from the city's cabarets. However, his girlie pages turned into the more sophisticated picture pages of the evening paper *Expressen* and launched the bandy player from Harnäs to a top position with TV.

Across the street at Norra Bantorget, the Social Democrats had ventured to start an afternoon paper, *Afton Tidningen* with Tore Nilsson heading the sports section. Tore was set for a great career and finally became head of the publishing company *Åhlén and Åkerlund* that produced three quarters of all magazines in Sweden. I knew

Tore from my struggling years. We met frequently at sports events. These were the days towards the end of the war when Gunder Hägg and Arne Andersson dominated the record tables from 800 to 10,000 meters. Tore and I decided to cash in on reader interest by writing columns for the newspapers around the country. Tore wrote Gunder's column and I wrote Arne Andersson's. Of course we shared the money, ten kronor per column per paper, with the athletes but we could not even whisper about that risking their disqualification. We called our endeavor the Gossip Bureau. I don't know why. We also supplied specials for local papers around the country when teams from their area played in Stockholm.

I needed the money now as a family man. Although Lill still worked we had our son Peter and a new apartment with monthly payments on new furniture. I was doing O.K. at NDA, however I knew that the paper was going to fold when Dagens Nyheter launched Expressen, its afternoon edition. I looked around to find a steady job with a local paper somewhere. *Örebro Dagblad* sounded great to me for the job as lead reporter - until I found that the conservative paper had great financial problems. Salaries were paid in portions whenever some advertiser paid. With the other three reporters we scheduled alternating free lunches at promotional events. I can hear the chief editor calling out, " Hi guys. Who is going to eat today?"

With my own family an old tradition came to an end - the Christmas Day dinners with veterinarian Martin Cronstrand's family in their magnificent apartment on Norrlandsgatan just around the corner from Stureplan.

As years passed into decades, the four children of the four Christmas families went from playing on the nursery floor to sharing musical and literary interests. The son of the house, Börje Cronstrand, developed an intense interest in opera. He took expensive voice lessons but we never heard him sing. He went around humming and talking about the air support. When he asked my father for advice my father said, "It's simple. If you have a pipe, use it." Börje ended up as an engineer with the Civil Aviation Board. However, he opened us up to the world of operas. He had record series of almost every recorded opera and a special player. His fascination with opera was, she has so admitted, the inspiration for his girl friend, Kjerstin Dellert. She became one of the greatest opera singers and popular entertainers in Sweden. While Kjerstin listened, Börje analyzed and dissected, Ulf Linde and I did not do much. We listened, probably a bit bored. Opera is of course entertaining but as with whipped cream, you can have too much. Ulf showed his intellectual capacities early. As a professor he ended up as a member of the Swedish Royal Academy and is one of the selectors for the Nobel Prize in literature. Kjerstin, who caused a scandal among gossipmongers when she married a vastly younger choreographer, shamed the critics by staying married. Today at just over 80, she devotes her days to her life interest - the Confidence, the Ulriksdals Castle royal theater that she dug out from a barn and seed store and brought back to it's 18th century magnificence. It is today one of the cultural gems of Sweden, thanks to Kjerstin.

During one of the starving days in Örebro I caught an ad for a position with *Östergötlands Dagblad* in Norrköping, a well-financed paper with a great reputation. I sent in a job application mentioning the many papers I had worked at but did not specify for how long. I was summoned for an interview and apparently I made a good impression. Of course whatever they asked me about my abilities to edit a paper, I totally convinced them of my proficiency.

I was supposed to start on a Monday. They called me in on Friday. The night editor that put the paper together and saw to it going to press was sick, so did I mind coming in. Did I mind?! I did not have a clue how to put a paper together. However, I had never backed out of a challenge and this was not the time to do it.

I found it in a bottle of rationed Swedish Aquavit called OP Andersson. Liquor was rationed in Sweden and hard to get. I took the big bottle with me to the paper that evening and went straight to the head of the typographical section that had worked the lead, as we called it, for years.

The true reasons for me getting the job were that the paper had recently had a fall out among the staff and that I was able to start right away. So I took my bottle to Svensson and said, "Svensson, my name is Ottoson, new at the paper and I have been asked to edit the weekend edition. I don't have a clue of how to do that. Please help me. Here is a bottle of OP Andersson. Svensson, with the Swedish title of 'färdiggörare' (make-ready) said, "Don't worry lad, we'll put out a paper."

I knew how to grade news and where it belonged. So when Svensson said he needed a 6-column 48-point headline, Garamond, down two on 36 and gave me a chart, I began to grasp it. Svensson was a better page creator than any night editor the paper had ever had.

The next day the chief editor Ivar Andersson of Svenska Dagbladet, who was the board chairman of Östergötlands Dagblad, called my chief editor Hadar Hadarsson and said, "Damn fine front page this morning. One of the best."

"Yes," said Hadarsson, "That new guy we just hired is pretty good."

I learned quickly and was lucky that the regular night editor came back after a couple of days. I grew into the job and took over after him when Dagens Nyheter hired him.

Lill, Peter and I were finally together as a family. We

had a nice apartment on Stora Nygatan. Lill took a job as an accountant at the hospital and we hired a young farmer's daughter to look after Peter and the home. I ran awful hours, starting work around eight in the evening and seldom coming home until three in the morning. There was, however, that very special feeling when I walked through the city at night with the paper in my pocket. I knew what had happened in the world and in the morning the city would wake up to read the news that I presented them.

The computerized newspaper people of today will never be able to feel how it is to sit and wait for a press to start. I had a 2:15 deadline for the press to start, which allowed time for loading on trains and busses. We could not afford to miss the train. So I sat there with a pot of coffee chain smoking and waiting... Three minutes to go! Nothing. Two minutes! Nothing. Now the seconds rolled. Thirty, twenty, ten and so, finally... The rumble of the press, the roar of it spitting out the papers! It was every night the same unbelievable feeling.

I believe that at the time I was the youngest night editor in Sweden in many a year. When, after a couple of months at the job, I confessed to Hadarsson, he laughed and said that I followed the golden rule of journalism, "Find your sources and hide your ignorance."

One day a young lean man fresh out of school showed up and asked me for a summer job at the paper. We needed a proofreader and I figured he would do the most good at that position. I knew he was disappointed but he took the job and regularly provided me with columns about nature that in most cases we failed to publish.

Bengt Danielsson did not look much like an adventurer to me, and still did not the day he told me that he was leaving the paper to go with a Norwegian expedition on a float called KonTiki to trace an historic peoples movement in the Pacific. He soon became Norrköping's most famous son.

Danielsson stayed for many years on Bora Bora in the Fiji archipelago in the Pacific. He became Swedish consul out there until he returned to Sweden as head of the Ethnographical Museum in Stockholm. He grew a beard the big unruly size of which made him look like a long time ship wrecked sailor.

Norrköping was the leading soccer city and speedway city in Sweden. It was the city of the Nordal brothers. Gunnar became the first Swedish soccer player to turn professional as he was hired as center forward of MC Milan in Italy. Often stomping into the sports editor's room was speedway world champ Varg Olle Nygren to see Bertil von Wachenfeldt who still held the Swedish record in 400 meters and was remembered as a hero since that evening in 1935 when he against all odds, led the Swedish relay team to Sweden's first athletic victory against Germany. It made the radio reporter Sven Jerring lose his voice and the King to scream with the masses at the Stockholm Station.

I came to love the sound of the start of a printing press. You work a full night and all that work is given to be typeset, framed, matrixed and made into lead halves for the press cylinders. You sit there staring at the clock waiting for the starting rumble of the press. Your feet come down from the desk when there is only a minute left, the ashtray full of cigarette stubs, all the coffee finished. Your feet hit the floor to balance you when the press finally starts rumbling sounding like a train that slowly accelerates across the rail sections. A journalist who has never listened to a printing press has missed the essence of the life of a newspaper.

IFK Norrköping in the 40's was undoubtedly the best soccer team in Sweden and I don't think it was ever surpassed. There were Knut and Gunnar Nordahl, Bian Rosengren, Mulle and Masse Holmquist, Åby Eriksson and Sweden's soccer goalie Torsten Lindberg. That team went over to England just after the war and beat the heck out of both Chelsea and Manchester United. I know. I saw them. The legendary Nalle Halldén who also became both coach and nominator for the Swedish national team managed the team.

A reminder of my years in Norrköping appeared 35 years later in Miami at a Swedish Chamber of Commerce luncheon for the Swedish Ambassador to Washington, Olof Thunborg. I kept looking at him and could not for my life remember where we had met before. I ventured to ask him. He looked at me and laughed and said, "You wrote a lot about me when I rode speedway for 'Vargarna' in Norrköping. An unusual career, don't you think?"

Right after the war I was sent on an assignment to war torn Finland, to the town of Joensu with which Norrköping had a sister city arrangement. Standing with general Snellman at what was the eastern-most frontier and one the Russians were never able to break through, I asked him how come, with the Finnish forces being outnumbered ten to one, this was possible.

"They learned to fear us during the winter," he said. "They could not grasp that these white clad figures who were gliding without a sound through the forest were anything but ghosts. But," he added, "we also nabbed and killed some Russians and put them on poles with big signs greeting attackers saying, 'Welcome to hell.' Superstitious as the Russians were they stayed behind their lines."

The reason for Finland's fierce resistance was that, when drafted a soldier was assigned to a front as close to his home as possible. Now on the Ilomants frontier the Finnish troops consisted mainly of men whose homes were just a few kilometers from the front.

I remember one farm where the only remaining building was the sauna. An old woman lived there while the men were at the front. General Snellman and I were invited in. The woman took out a jar of raspberries and wanted us to eat as it was all she had to offer and in Finland hospitality demanded that you offer a guest something for his palate. The general saw that I was about to say no thank you to the raspberries. "You have to eat it or she'll be offended." It felt almost bizarre to stand there in a sauna eating the only thing the woman could offer and looking at her smiling face, satisfied that she had a gift for her guests.

Back from the Ilomants front I spent some time in Helsinki, which at the time was under Russian occupation. From the Finnish military office, the 9-year-old son of general Snellman guided me back to my hotel. On the way I took pictures of Russian soldiers. All the way back to the hotel the boy did not say a word. As I thanked him at the hotel he only said, "If I had a fine camera like that I would not waste film on Russians."

I had been three years in Norrköping and considered other job opportunities that would give me more flexible work. As it was I was mostly tied down to editing work and was only occasionally given assignments like the one to Finland. Then one day I was told that the British embassy in Stockholm was looking for a reporter to the BBC's Swedish section in London.

I applied and received time for an interview with the British press attaché John Leadbetter. I was not very good in English so on the train to Stockholm I prepared myself by formulating answers to questions I presumed he would ask. Fortunately he spoke Swedish so the interview backed by my prepared phrases went well. However, he wanted to give me a written test and gave me an editorial to translate from the London Times. And if anything, the editorials in Times are highbrow enough even for British to understand some times. As I studied the article I recognized that it dealt with the same subject as Svenska Dagbladet had commented on a couple of days before and we had quoted extensively in my paper and to which I had even added a foot note. As I was unable to translate the very sophisticated English I picked up whatever was easiest to translate and sort of commented on the rest. I explained to Leadbetter that I presumed that British press commentaries to be transmitted should perhaps be adapted for the Swedes who were not necessarily familiar with the problem.

"I feel", I said, "that a comment or explanation is more appropriate for a transmission to Sweden than a translation."

"Excellent!" replied Leadbetter. "That's exactly the way it's meant to be."

I got the job there and then.

There is a Swedish expression 'tur som en tokig' (lucky as a fool) and that was so true once again.

The war was hardly over. The British still picked up ball bearings by torpedo boats or converted Lincoln bombers from the SKF factory in Gothenburg. SKF helped to keep the British wheels turning all through the war.

One day I found myself on board one of these converted Lincoln bombers on my way to London.

LONDON TIMES

An unforgettable day in March of 1946 I stepped into that converted Lincoln bomber at Bromma airport in Stockholm and flew to England.

We landed at Heathrow Airport where I had to walk through a row of five round roofed steel barracks - one for immigration, one for customs, one for health control, one for waiting and one for the bus to the city. It was a rainy day when I arrived so I was able to get wet four times. Since then, I have landed umpteen times at Heathrow but never seen it finished. It must be one of the world's most drawn out building projects. I bet it will never be finished.

Bush House on Aldwych, between Strand and Fleet Street was the home during the war for about forty foreign radio sections. The building teemed with exiled kings, presidents and ministers. The Swedish section was sort of a stepchild and assigned only half an hour of airtime a day.

I was paid seven guineas a week, which was equivalent to seven pounds and seven shillings. This is an excellent illustration of how the British are experts at complicating the simplest things. Guinea was used to separate the fine from the average. Thus a fur coat would be priced in guineas but a raincoat in pounds. A Rolex would be priced in guineas but a Timex in pounds. We at the BBC were paid in Guineas but the police constable directing the traffic outside Bush House was paid in pounds. I think this is a perfect illustration of how the British can simplify difficult problems and complicate simple ones.

I had a couple of months to wait before Lill could join me. British immigration had to do a search of her background before issuing a visa for her and Peter. When the Swedish section of the BBC needed a reporter, the Foreign Office found it to be an emergency enough to bring me over by military plane. When it came to my family that was no emergency. After all, it was only the family of a foreigner.

I found a room with an old couple in Maidavale. She was an old chain-smoking lady who collected picture postcards of royalty and her husband was an army retiree. The fat lady and her retired husband with a bomber command mustache and sort of a voice to go with a noncommissioned officer in Her Majesty's Rifles were my new landlords. In slippers and a half smoked cigarette, her favorite place was the ladies' room at the Rose and Crown. One night she invited me to look at her collection of postcards of royalties. When, after a while I asked her if she might have one of Mrs. Simpson, she gave me an ice-cold look and said, "Mr. Ottoson I think it's time for you to go to bed now."

In the British effort to simplify the difficult - unless they have come up with a more complicated system lately - is was necessary to run the water pipes on the outside walls of buildings and to allow the overflow holes of bathtubs to empty right out in the air. Of course they argue that it is very practical to have the pipes outside so they can be easily repaired in case they freeze. Not yet aware of the English plumbing hazards, I filled up the tub for a bath.

There was soon a bang on the bathroom door followed by my landlady's stern voice,

"Mr. Ottoson. What are you doing in there?"

"Taking a bath."

"I know that, but you are flooding my coal box!"

The overflow pipe from the tub emptied right outside the wall. The water ran down the wall and happened to flow into the kitchen coal box and in turn onto the kitchen steps.

"If Mr. Ottoson intends to take a full bath, I suggest that Mr. Ottoson goes to the beach at Brighton."

When she inspected the bathroom afterwards and found that the floor was wet, all she could say was,

"Brighton, Mr. Ottoson, Brighton."

At night it was very cold in the room because like all British fireplaces they had no damper so the moment the fire burned out the outside weather moved in. Maybe they found it easier with bed warmers than with dampers. The low nativity in England certain times of the year is said to have a direct relation to bed warmers. The British-Hungarian writer and humorist George Mikes put it this way, "Continental people have a sex life. Englishmen use hot water bottles."

Mikes worked for the Hungarian section in Bush House in a room next to mine. He looked like a twin brother of the actor Peter Lorre. He became one of the most popular humorist writers in England during the forties and fifties.

His first book How to be an Alien began thus:

"I have been an alien all my life except that during my first 25 years in Budapest I was not aware of it."

To be a foreigner, that is to say "a bloody foreigner," in England before the Second World War was something unsavory, almost obscene. Right after the war, certain exceptions could be made for some members of the Commonwealth. Eastern was quite obscene provided you were not from any of the countries from the Garlic belt, (Spain, Italy, Greece....) or from Eastern Europe. Scandinavians were almost accepted. They were promoted from bloody foreigners to plain foreigners. An Englishman traveling abroad never regarded himself as a foreigner. He was just surrounded by foreigners. When the telephone cable under the English Channel malfunctioned, the London Times headline read: Continent cut off!

I was fully aware that I had to improve my English to be able to translate all the telegrams and editorials. I was given a week to adapt to London life and spent most of the time watching British films. I saw each film three times and each time I understood more of what was said on the screen. What I did not understand the first run I might know the second time and definitely understood the third time.

How bad was my English? It was so bad in fact that I translated the British general staff with the British General Staff.

Head man of the Swedish section was a tall lean London Swede, Halvor William Olsson. Under him worked a motley crew of Swedish journalists. There was the former chief editor of Sydsvenska Dagbladet, Pierre Backman and the Christian daily Svenska Morgonbladet's London correspondent Bengt Hallström, and the film expert and future head of Svenska Film Institutet, Torsten Jungstedt. Strict in form was Håkan Unsgård who later advanced to head Sveriges Radio in Stockholm. They were all great to work with - men with talents and their own ideas. There may sometimes have been a little too much talent in one place.

Even though the transmissions were for only half an hour we had time to run headline news, commentaries for ten minutes and could fill the rest with interviews, film and theater talk, arts events etc. Britain did not need to broadcast the same vivid propaganda to Sweden as to, for instance, the countries behind the iron curtain. It was also here that Torsten Jungstedt got the idea for the radio series The Man in Black which he later so successfully took to the Swedish Radio.

How many listened to us in Sweden? We used to jokingly say, "Maybe we don't need to send tonight because our listener has gone to the movies." But we had in fact about 100,000 listeners. One of the most true was Dagens Nyheter's feared radio critic Karin Schultz who used us to hit Sveriges Radio. She wrote and suggested that Sveriges Radio send for Lars Henrik Ottoson and Torsten Jungstedt to get some decent programs.

Both Torsten and I had ambitions to get jobs with Swedish Radio when our four-year contracts expired. But we were not very popular at Kungsgatan for being clubs with which Karin Schultz attacked the Swedish national radio. I never made it. Torsten made it by marrying the daughter of the director of the radio organization, Yngve Hugo. Unsgård made it because he stayed low doing mostly news. He came into the organizing side of the state owned enterprise. I was eliminated from any consideration for a job in Stockholm the day Karin Schultz presented me with a photo in Dagens Nyheter as Sweden's best radio reporter. It meant that my last potato was planted in Sweden.

Some of my finest memories from London are thanks to Torsten. He never ceased to surprise me with his literary and cinematic knowledge and his humor that was more Uppsala than the British could consume. Once he went on a tour on the Thames with a group of journalists invited by the Navy. He joked about the ship and meant it would be great to have one for fishing. The navy complained to the BBC and Jungstedt was called to the head of the BBC foreign division. Torsten just laughed and said,

"So they did not like it. I'll tell you what! I'll start a collection among frustrated BBC reporters for buying one of those tubs for fishing."

Torsten surprised Charlie Chaplin in an interview by knowing more about his film crews than the master knew himself. Because of this knowledge, he invited Torsten Jungstedt to his home in Switzerland. Another of Jungstedt's admirers was George Bernhard Shaw. Torsten arrived one day with a photographer at Shaw's home in Ireland. Unannounced he knocked on the door.

"Mr. Shaw is not at home," said the housekeeper who opened the door.

"Sure he is," said Torsten. "He is just behind that curtain peeking at me."

Shaw thought that was funny so he came out and asked how Torsten could know that.

"I did not," said Torsten, " but old men are curious and I bet you were no different." Shaw laughed and they had a walk in the garden where Torsten had hidden his photographer. When Shaw bent down to pat a cat he sort of stumbled - one leg up in the air. That photo sold all over the world for big money.

I think Halvor William Olsson, who was a bit of a dreamer, hired Torsten because he saw in him a bit of himself - a creative dreamer. One day before lunch in the staff canteen, Torsten as usual went to the toilet by the entrance. Except this time he walked into the ladies room. A change of toilets was prominently displayed but Torsten never read signs. So he did what he was supposed to do and after washing his hands he looked for a towel. There was nothing but a dispenser that said "Sanitary Towels" six pence.

He cursed a bit for having to pay. He pulled out a package. He got a safety pin and thought that could be practical and put it in his pocket as he started to unwrap the "towel." While standing there looking at it a couple of women came in, saw Torsten, screamed and ran. Torsten was called for investigation and the head of the Foreign Services fumed,

"Are you not that Swede who was going to buy a naval ship for fishing? Get out of my sight!"

At the time, BBC was the world's largest radio organization with more than fifteen thousand employees.

And think about it! This little Swedish section had the use of all the enormous company resources. Whatever I wanted to do or wherever I wanted to go, all I had to do was to call Mrs. Peacock of Traffic for train tickets, hotel rooms, recording vans etc. In 1948 for the Olympics I had a permanent seat in the radio section at Wembley Stadium and convinced Halvor to strengthen the sports team with Bertil von Wachenfeldt during the Games. I even used Lennart Hyland from Sveriges Radio as guest a couple of times. BBC paid him a pound a minute.

London after the war was this enormously big dirty lady in rags and tatters, a fascinating city through which the Thames tumbled its muddy waters towards the sea. The Eros statue at Piccadilly Circus was covered not against bomb damage, but to prevent foreign soldiers on leave in London from climbing on it for snapshots. The rules were a little more liberal at Trafalgar Square where Nelson rode his horse. There were so many equestrian statues in London that the city allowed a freer use of them.

I needed to save some money for the arrival of Lill and Peter. The first extra job was as an assistant to the London Correspondent of Svenska Dagbladet, T.G. Wickbom. It was not much more than watching his telephone at London Times where Svenska Dagbladet had a room and news service. As the Swedish transmission ended at 8 and Times was just at the other end of Fleet Street, I could be there by 9. I also got the job of editing a Swedish edition of the Fox Movietone Newsreel that played before the films at cinemas in Sweden. I made more than a hundred of them over the years. The London Times sort of displayed it's snobbery towards the rest of the many papers in London by not being on Fleet Street but a couple of hundred meters away just within the walls of the City. T.G. Wickbom for *Svenska Dagbladet* and Agne Hamrin for *Dagens Nyheter* were the two journalists who provided Swedish readers with the most informed and balanced world news. TG worked out of a room at the Times in the light of a bulb dangling from the ceiling. He had two chairs, a desk, a telephone and a Remington typewriter. Twice a day he received the proofs from Times news desk for tomorrow's paper.

T G Wickbom was one of the best-ever Swedish foreign correspondents. Even though Samuel Johnson said that if you are tired of London you are tired of life, TG never tired of London but of the primitive conditions under which he had to work. I think he was also a bit too independent to enter the editorial togetherness in Stockholm. He broke loose and took a job as information director and a very independent one with Grängesberg, a mining company with big stakes in Liberia.

When SS Saga arrived from Gothenburg and moored below Tower Bridge, Swedish Lloyd's PR vice president Bengt Malm became much sought after. In exchange for filling us with Swedish food in a harshly rationed Britain, we served as guides to his prominent guests. Mostly it was I who provided the service because as I was still living single I had the time and a reporter's nose for the dark places.

One day Malm put a top looking lady in my care, Britt Kolming, a furniture merchant's daughter from Gothenburg. She planned to stay in London for a couple of months for the language and atmosphere. Did I have "honorable intentions?" Of course not. She was too good looking and sexy for that. However, I did not get very far because I made the mistake (thank God) to take her to the Coconut Grove night club on Regent Street to listen and dance to Edmundo Ros Orchestra - Edmundo owned the place and his band was at the time the most popular band in Europe. As we danced Britt gave him some loving eye apparently. He came to our table and I was sort of out of the picture within ten minutes. That was the beginning of an intense courtship that lasted for a month, until they got married. I took Britt to the club every night and they drove me home in Edmundo's Rolls Royce at 3 a.m. When Edmundo took a break and came over to our table, the cigarette girl, who was also a looker, came over to keep me company. She was engaged to a gardener in Richmond and the tips she received all went from her bra into the ground out there. Seven pounds, seven shillings a week was not much money when half had to go to rent. So the Fox Movietone Newsreel was a blessing. Thus thousands of Swedes from Ystad to Haparanda had heard my voice years before television.

Closing in on the day Peter and Lill would arrive I found a so called mews flat on Harley Street close to the main BBC building and the Swedish embassy. A mews was sort of a back alley for horses and carriages in the old days but was now pretty fashionable. The place still had some cracks in the walls from the bombing. You could see the sky through a crack in the upstairs sitting room. With no damper in the fireplace it created a bit of a cross draft at night. In the bedroom I hung an electric heater in the ceiling above the bed.

"What is that?" asked Lill.

"It's the English version of central heating," I said as we put on clothes to go to bed.

Lill was on her hands and knees scrubbing the kitchen floor when she called me, totally frustrated, complaining that this was the dirtiest filthiest floor she had ever seen.

"I have used three buckets of water and all turned black. I don't know what to do!"

"Do nothing," I said. "You are scrubbing dirt. This is the old dirt floor of the stable."

Mansfield Mews was convenient for me. I could walk to Bush House in forty-five minutes but it was not much of a family place. We finally found a modern apartment - modern according to the British, in Chiswick, a suburb close to Kew Gardens. One reason that it was available was that it had central heating and no fireplaces. Englishmen in those days did not like the dry heat of central heating and they were all surprised when I showed them that you could turn it off or moderate it. We enrolled Peter in the local school and he got his first school uniform. It was winter and cold when he came running home crying because the other kids made fun of his golf trousers. He refused to go back to school unless he could have short pants like everyone else. Blue frozen knees or not. One day he came home early saying they had closed the school for a couple of days because "we can't excuse ourselves." In other words the toilets were frozen.

A proud day in my life was when a boy came to our door to give Peter a cricket bat.

"Thank you," I said, " but what are you to have?"

"Oh, I have a grown up one's now."

"But Peter can't play cricket," I added.

"Oh yes, sir, he can almost bowl straight now."

What a thing to tell my friends in London. I had a son who could bowl straight in cricket!

Lill had been pregnant for a while and we had made arrangements with a nursing home in Richmond for when the day came. When it did, there was no taxi so Lill said, "Let's take the bus." We had no choice. It would normally be about half an hour's ride. After ten minutes Lill's water broke. The conductor told the driver who put the pedal to the floor, passed all stops horn blaring and out of the route and finally swung up in front of the nursing home to the wild cheers of the other passengers, saying proudly, "We made it luv."

When I came back the next day a nurse put Lillebil Kristina Larsdotter in my arms before I had even removed my wet overcoat. Outside a couple of pregnant women were running around a fountain. At this hospital expectant mothers had to come in the day the doctor had set for the delivery. To achieve the wanted results he then fed them castor oil and made them run. I asked how often they cleaned the place.

"You are crazy," said Lill, "they don't clean, they wax."

With Lill and the baby the rations became manageable. When I lived alone I had coupons for half a liter of milk and two eggs a week and ten shillings worth of meat including breakfast bacon. Often I missed buying the rations because the waiting lines were too long. That's when I discovered the horsemeat shop. Horsemeat was only allowed to be sold in special shops and was for dog consumption. In Sweden we often ate smoked horsemeat. And I was hungry. I became a weekly customer of the shop and asked for special cuts. The butcher finally looked at me and asked, " What kind of dog do you have? Does he use a knife and fork?"

NUREMBERG

I had not been long with the BBC when I was asked to follow the development of the criminal war court in Nuremberg. The American prosecutor Robert Jackson had assembled a group of colleagues including Nikitchenko from Russia and Robert Falco from Great Britain. Twenty-one German leaders were on trial from the German military and civilian war machinery - a group considered to have carried the main responsibility for the Nazi war crimes and crimes against humanity.

I took an intense interest in the proceedings and as

the tribunal was closing in on its final phase, I wanted to be there on judgment day. However, there was so much going against me. I was too young and too inexperienced for a world historic event of this magnitude. Also I represented one of the minor BBC foreign sections and there was no money in my section's budget for such a massive outlay.

When I talked with my boss and he with his boss they both came to the same conclusion: Forget it. This is for the big boys.

In all large bureaucracies there is always someone a step or two under the big boss level who can arrange things effectively and unknown by anyone. Among the 13,000 BBC employees it was Miss Peacock of Traffic. She was the one who fixed tickets and money for the foreign sections. I made sure that I bumped into her at lunchtime in the canteen and helped clear a place for her. She was very busy arranging a Nuremberg trip for a couple from the Russian section. When I approached her about it she just smiled. I still bumped into her in the cafeteria and I worked totally neutral conversations with her to find out what she was interested in. One day she said what a shame it was that the family could never have a real good Sunday steak together. Bingo! I rushed to contact my friend Svenska Lloyds PR director. I told him I needed a big steak for six as a ticket to Nuremberg. He came up with it. I put it in Miss Peacock's car and I did not have to say anything.

"Oh dear oh dear," she said, "Now I guess I have to take the Turk off the list."

A reporter from the French section and his wife were driving to Germany and I was going with them, as public transportation was still shaky and unreliable on the Continent. The car was a two-seater with an extra seat, a so-called rumble seat, mainly meant for baggage. You opened it up and the lid became the back of a seat. It was a bit cramped until I could convince the Frenchman to move some of the luggage to the top of the car.

We had been driving an hour or two past Calais when it started to rain. And DID it rain! I felt like sitting in a bucket being filled until we were able to secure a piece of canvas from a British army unit. We made a hole in the canvas for my head and draped me in the rest. The roads were almost all like wide strings of mud and potholes as we plowed our way towards Germany. The closer we came to the German border, the more damaged were the French cities that we passed. Until in Germany they just did not exist three feet above the ground. We crossed the border at Koenigswusterhausen where people were living like moles under ground. When there was a building left you might be able to secure a bed for the night for half a piece of soap and a meal for 3 or 4 cigarettes.

From an article in the *Post Journal*, Jamestown, N.Y., February 13, 2002:

Celebration of Justice—Swedish Born News Reporter Remembers Nuremberg Trials

The evening before the 110th anniversary of the birth of Justice H. Jackson, the Center dedicated to preserving his memory hosted a talk by Swedish born journalist Lars H. Ottoson who covered the proceedings of the International Military Tribunal at Nuremberg for the Swedish Service of the British Broadcasting Corporation. Ottoson spoke to an audience of over 100 people after a dinner. Ottoson said that Nuremberg was "a fair victor's tribunal" and he was very impressed by the directness of Justice Jackson. "What he did was to lay the foundation of the principle that superior orders are not a defense for war crimes, a rule that stands today at the tribunal in Hague. That was Jackson's greatness."

How come the Allied selected Nuremberg over Munich, the birthplace of the Nazi movement? A tribunal in Munich might have felt like a knife pushed into the Nazi soul. But Nuremberg was the showplace of the Nazi movement where Hitler spoke to thousands of party members and the place from which the world saw him in all his power. By chance or on purpose - who knows - the fact is that the main buildings in the town had been saved from destruction and had enough room to house tribunal offices and prison areas.

The journalists were housed at Schloss Farben in Leverkusen. The castle belonged to the Bayer family of Aspirin fame. Bayer was at the time the world's largest chemical and medical supplier.

When I sit here writing or travel in this security conscious world and think back to the time in Nuremberg, it seems almost unbelievable that all I needed to get into the tribunal offices and courtroom was an ID card which was checked against a list at the entrance. No frisking, no search in bags. I could easily have walked right in with a bomb hidden in my typewriter cover. But of course in those days you didn't do things like that. It was not kosher.

What struck me when I sat there perhaps fifty feet from the 21 accused was how miserable they all looked robbed of both power and uniforms. These were, after all, men who wherever they went had represented power. For instance, the presence of von Papen or Ribbentrop would have completely dominated his surroundings. Now they were just a bunch of tired old men. The same impression held true for all the others like the field marshals Jodel, Keitel and Raeder. Robbed of their uniforms and all the medals, they did not look much different from the old men they hated - the aged Jews on the verandas in Miami Beach.

Then of course there was Hermann Goering, the contrast. He had lost a lot of weight so his jacket hung on him like a blanket. Still he commanded some form of respect. He might have been one of the worst war criminals, the creator of the Gestapo and the concentration camps. The respect shown him came from the fact that he admitted his crimes. "Yes I did it. Yes I ordered it." He was the only one to openly state his guilt.

We know that Hermann Goering committed suicide only hours before he was to be hung. To this day there is still the unsolved mystery of how he could get the cyanide tablets. We journalists speculated a lot about the possibility that one of the U.S. guards had supplied the pills. We knew that the American guards liked Hermann Goering and were often seen in conversation with him. He was the only prisoner who did not wear handcuffs when outside his cell.

Hermann Goering was one of Germany's flying aces in the First World War. In the twenties he spent a lot of time in Sweden and he married a Swedish girl. He also advised the Swedish military on creating an air force. He trained many Swedish pilots.

In the courtroom he sat fairly relaxed with his right arm resting on a side rail. To his left sat Rudolf Hess, tense, hollow eyed, ghostly.

The old broken men all sat there with fisted hands and without moving, but I understood that back in the cell block many of them were shouting at each other about who was most to blame for the outcome of the war. This was especially true for Field Marshal Raeder and Admiral Dönitz. The fight between them went on furiously on the prison yard in Berlin for eleven years after the tribunal. It was all about who was the most responsible for Germany losing the war. Eighteen times the words "death by hanging" rang out in the courtroom. Even here Hermann Goering handled himself with poise. When he came out of the elevator flanked by two GIs he wore no handcuffs, the only one so allowed. He raised his right hand as if greeting us in the press box. When the guards put on his headphones to hear the translation into German of his sentence he raised his hand and shook his head. Apparently the headphones malfunctioned. The guards got him a new pair. Now he put thumbs up. The words he could hear were "death by hanging."

Twenty-one men were on trial. Eighteen received the death penalty. In all that has been written about the rise and fall of the Third Reich, no one has ever asked how this could happen. How could we allow the world to be duped after Hitler had invaded Austria, occupied Saar and Sudetenland? How could we believe this man's pledge of peace after he received what he wanted through the Munich Accords? When conservative then Prime Minister of England, Neville Chamberlain declared "peace in our time" to the wild cheers of the public welcoming the delegation on their return from Munich, the French were shaking their heads. Winston Churchill was not duped but was heckled in Parliament when on its floor he warned against the menace of Hitler. The House answered Churchill that with words like that, it was he who threatened the peace.

Europe at the time had very little with which to stop Hitler plus the fact that he had many admirers including the larger part of the Swedish officers corps.

Europe loves uniforms and parades. It was an old admiration dating back to the times that a young man needed a uniform. The courts of Europe - and there were plenty of them - were filled with young officers in lavish uniforms. They all talked about finding a war in which to display their heroism. In England the oldest son in a family with any social ambitions was expected to become an officer and hopefully be able to serve in the colonies and just as hopefully find an opportunity to honor his uniform by hacking down some protesting insurgents. We had old traditions of the same kind in Sweden, ever since Gustav II Adolf and Karl XII perfected his swordsmanship by riding in a coral slashing the heads of horses.

Europe at first actually regarded Hitler as an asset for Germany. He had the trains running on time and every German had a job after the catastrophic Weimar Republic. Then there was Mussolini who made the trains in Italy run on time and Franco was their ideology brother in Spain. And the most expensive uniform tailors in Europe had a renaissance.

The uniform craze also hit the children. There were the brown shirts of the Nazi youth movements from North Cape to the Italian border where Mussolini's black shirts took over. I mean these guys were no boy scouts, a movement that suffered as teenagers were drawn to the military drills and weapons training in the dictatorial countries. What amazes me to this day is how one of the biggest Nazi parties to grow in England under Mosley, like Quisling in Norway and Sven Olof Lindholm in Sweden existed on German money.

Great Britain won the war but lost the Empire. Ten years after the end of WWII there was hardly anything of it left but a couple of small islands here and there. At BBC we inserted in our newscasts selected pieces that would show how Great Britain had planned this commonwealth solution for a long time. Somewhere we found something Winston Churchill had said some time in the twenties that "Albion's greatest moment will come the day when the colonies can rise and take the responsibility of governing themselves."

I remember the day in August of 1947 when I reported

the independence of India. On the back of the telegram that I had translated into Swedish, a guy at the news room had written, "Don't feel sorry for Great Britain but for the poor Indian devils who now have to face the task of taking care of themselves."

It was as if Britain wanted the world to believe that the disintegration of the Empire was part of a well-planned process to help its colonies to self-government.

America's isolationistic politics until it joined the war had for a long time prevented Great Britain from seriously considering the USA as a world-governing partner. England WAS the world run and governed from Downing Street, the Parliament and the City of London. Or maybe even more correctly by the products of two schools: Winchester and Eton. These two institutions dating back almost to the Middle Ages had survived attacks from Henry VIII, Cromwell, Victorian reformists and two world wars. The continuity with which pupils from these two schools climbed to power has no equivalent anywhere else in the world.

As late as 1982 half of Britain's government members were from these two schools, including the Foreign and Interior Ministers. Cabinet secretaries came from these schools and so did the presidents of the four largest banks, the majority of the country's judges and the heads of BBC and London Times.

Such a lasting dominance must have had a lasting impact on Britain's anatomy. Or as the analytical expert Anthony Heartly wrote, "It seems as if Eton and Winchester are conspiracies instead of learning places."

A narrow elite can of course never represent a whole people. They and their successes if I can call it that are more mirrored in restraint together with the preservation of status quo than by entering into industrial and political adventures. Their values were, I think, more related to the banking business and military activities than technology and industry. The British actually succeeded in taking apart its empire without political revolt but found it much harder to change the social structure to secure a strong commercial future.

The relatively financial well being during the fifties was not because of the British. With already an old and worn out machine park, England was able to compete in the world market because they had no competition. It worked despite constant equipment breakdowns and strikes.

Eton and Winchester occupied the boardrooms. Figures from the House of Lords, often totally useless figures, occupied the board rooms while Germany and Japan put people to work 12-15 hours a day with brand new machinery and new techniques. So Albion just slumped in most fields and it has taken almost fifty years for Britain to catch up on the world market. However, it is not so much the merit of the Englishmen as it is foreign investors, especially Americans that have established European bridgeheads in England and the international finance market that has made the City of London a center for world finance. Today over half of the Swedish industries have boards with links in London.

England during the years after the war reminded me about the story of the retired colonel reading the London Times in his favorite chair in the exclusive Army and Navy Club in London. He sees David Niven who was an officer once in the ranking regiment the Queens Rifles before becoming an actor. The colonel spots him.

"Hello Niven. Haven't seen you for ages. Where have you been?"

"In Hollywood, sir."

"Oh... where is that?"

"On the west coast of America, sir."

"My God Niven, I didn't know we had troops stationed out there."

AIR/SEA RESCUE

When the head of the Scandinavian section called me in one day and asked me to sign a life insurance policy for a job, I figured it had to be an important one. He said it was for a very special job - and I believed him. I was going to go to sea with the Navy and when on board I'd be told what it encompassed. Lill was not too happy about not knowing why I had to have a life insurance for doing a job at sea with the navy. But I was pretty excited

Now afterwards I realized it was not such a big deal, but it all came together as so very British that I can't hold it back from you.

A naval officer picked me up at the train station in Plymouth and took me to a destroyer at the Colshot naval base south of town. He did not want to talk about anything but the ongoing cricket game against Australia at the Lords in London.

Well on board I was shown to a cabin and told to make myself comfortable and come to the officers' mess at eighteen hundred. So I did. I had a rather chilly reception. Obviously these officers did not look forward to having a civilian mixed into whatever they planned to do.

It was - you guessed it - cricket talk until 20 hundred when a wing commander advised me to go to bed because there was going to be an early morning. A wing commander on a naval ship was my first clue of what was planned. Back in my cabin I found a heavy pilot's uniform, big boots and an inflatable vest. I was told to be dressed and ready by 5 hundred. An ensign brought me a cup of coffee and a biscuit.

I said to myself that they were going to throw me in the drink. Why me? I learned later that the BBC had difficulties finding a reporter who was physically fit, young and a good swimmer. The British live surrounded by water but they don't swim much.

The Captain informed me that I was going to take part in an air sea rescue event with a bomber dropping a lifeboat. He said that he had strongly protested against inserting a civilian in the operation, however the Admiralty insisted on having a BBC reporter participating. There was enough military secrecy in the world, but here was a chance for Britain to show off in a very neutral way.

The water in the English Channel was pretty choppy, three to four feet. The destroyer was heaving a bit and we were told to jump when it heaved starboard. Wing Commander Horner, two air force lieutenants and I jumped and swam away from the ship. I heard the captain on his megaphone, "Good luck gentlemen." Slowly the destroyer backed away from us not to cause propeller draft.

The destroyer took off. I was alone with three air force officers playing ship wrecked. I had blown up my inflatable vest, the air bag that kept my head above water. Horner pulled out a rope and tied us on to it. I mean even if you play ship wrecked it was no reason to overdo it according to Horner.

We floated for a couple of hours. Horner said the bomber had better come soon because it seemed that one of those infamous Channel fogs started creeping in on us. Every fifteen minutes Horner sent up a flare. Oh, my God I thought how are they going to find us if that fog buries us from view? But suddenly there it was - a big Lancashire bomber with a rescue boat strapped under it. It made a couple of turns around us and then coming straight at us dumped the lifeboat from 15 feet against the wind for it to drift towards us. The ability to move, even less to swim and to climb up in a boat when you are dressed like a Michelin figure was frustrating. I remember Horner grabbing my back and hauling me in.

I thought that now we just waited for the destroyer

to pick us up. But no. That was not in the plans. There were a lot of things to test onboard. Horner rigged a sail and set off for the French coast. The destroyer and a corvette now circled us at a distance much in order to warn other seafarers of our existence. Now and then they let off the foghorn and Horner signaled back. Signaled back, that is, until he got tired. He meant that under real circumstances there were no rescuers. He decided to sail to Le Havre. The navy foghorns became more and more distant and there we were alone in the fog.

Horner asked me, " Why do you take an assignment like this?"

"Because I was told."

"My God, I did not know that the military ran the BBC."

"Not the real BBC - only us bloody foreigners."

It sort of broke the ice or the tenseness that had existed. We were now sailing towards Le Havre. All through the night we had occasionally heard naval foghorns during the search for us.

We had done a lousy navigation job because the city we looked at in the distance was not Le Havre but St. Lo in Normandy. It was good that one of the officers discovered that the compass on the lifeboat was wrongly calibrated. Far in the distance the destroyer had caught sight of us. As it came closer Horner threw out a fishing line, sat back and relaxed. The captain in the most British of manners enquired,

"Wing Commander Horner, good morning Sir. Have you caught anything?"

"Not yet sir, we lost two. And thought we had lost you too."

I now thought we would get back on the ship, but Horner felt that he had to repair his navigational reputation by sailing us back to Plymouth by way of Le Havre, because Horner was a stubborn man.

I soon became accustomed to the new surroundings in England. Here I am in meetings and conversations with Prime Minister Edward Heath.

LARS-HENRIK OTTOSON

FORD, USA AND HOLLYWOOD

When my contract with the BBC ran out I could look back not just at the BBC but at so many other journalistic activities with Fox Movietone, Svenska Dagbladet and of writing the first Swedish guide books after the war. The first was Here is London that was co written by Pierre Backman. Then followed Here is England, ..Scotland, ..Wales.

The Swedish Lloyd provided the best link with Britain. You went by ship from Gothenburg across the North Sea and up the Thames to anchor just below the Tower Bridge. All so convenient—never a problem with hotel accommodations or meals.

Then, as the Swedes opened up Europe by bus I wrote a guide book telling them what they saw on different routes across the continent as the bus rolled among cathedrals, museums and hotels, By Bus Through Europe. The Swedes had been locked in the country for so long that they were bursting to get out.

I had advanced plans to write a book about a trip around the world but my father's health was waning so I decided to accept a job offer as advertising and public relations manager for Ford in Sweden. Ford Motor Company had an office and assembly plant by 'Frihamnen' (outside of customs) in Stockholm. From my office window I could watch the amphibious Junker planes take off for Helsinki, Finland. This was a steady nine to five job that made me gain almost 40 pounds and become a frequent visitor entertaining guests at the finest restaurants in town. I got the job after Claes Livijn who freelanced as radio disc jockey when he became president of the clothing company Junex.

We found a nice roomy apartment in Västertorp in the south end of Stockholm. We had a nice home, no debts, two cars and a simple job for someone who had never known an 8-hour working day with Saturdays off.

The line at the Ford plant assembled three models: The British Anglia, German Taunus and French Vedette. Swedish Ford was a subsidiary of Ford in England, which meant that the president, Otto Brøndum had British board visitors several times a year. I saw those British mainly at the Grand Hotel, the Operakällaren restaurant and Riche's bar. They were the typical titled British board members that I have described earlier. But they fit Otto Brøndum like a glove. He ran the company as if it was his own private enterprise. He did a great job and established excellent relations with the dealers, as he knew how to wine and dine them. He was sly too. He had a small monthly supply of American Fords. He had difficulties selling the Vedette that dominated the assembly line, so he quoted the dealers one American Ford for the sale of five Vedettes and two Anglias.

I worked with the advertising agencies and the press. One of my main assignments was to arrange dinners during the Ford Dealer Association's quarterly meetings and for board members with ladies. They were " four wine dinners" as I called them, starring some of Sweden's best entertainers.

It was sort of a segregated work place. There was a lunchroom for Brøndum and the heads of finance, sales and plant. There was another lunchroom with service naturally for heads of sections like trucks, engines, office operations and of course PR. Below that there was a meal room, or whatever you could call it, for the office staff and another for the factory people. Everyone was assigned a number giving an idea about his or her standing in the company. I had number four. Stepping ahead of both the office manager and the head of trucks became a bit of a problem. One reason that I got this job, regarded as a plum in the trade, was that the Brøndums had a summer home at Hasseludden outside Stockholm where my parents had a small weekend cottage. Otto B. and my father spent many summer evenings with drinks on the Brøndum porch. However, it was soon established that I was the right man for the job. After a couple of months the company sent me to America to learn about a new American invention called public relations.

The only things that are cheaper today than fifty years ago are airline tickets. My fare to New York in 1950 was, if I remember correctly, over $2,000.

I boarded a DC 4 at Bromma. We first went to Copenhagen, then on to Shannon in Ireland and across the ocean to Gander, Newfoundland where we had to be de-iced before continuing to La Guardia in New York. The plane was taken to a de-frosting hangar. Although it prolonged the trip for several hours, it was a welcome break to stretch your legs. During the flight I had been over to first class a couple of times to talk with an old friend, Sixten Ehrling. We roomed for a short while in London where he played an awesome boogie-woggie and jazz when relaxing from his classical routine. Now he was with Jussi Björling on the way to a concert in New York. Sixten walked over to a piano in the waiting room and asked Jussi, "Do you want to clean your pipes?" And there we were, about fifty passengers getting a free Jussi Björling concert. He went through a lot of scales aside from pieces from Tosca and La Traviata.

Sixten had a remarkable career. Starting at the Opera in Stockholm as a rehearsal pianist for the ballet, he became a concert pianist, conductor of the Royal Opera, Conductor to the Royal Court, Conductor first for the Chicago and then for the Detroit Symphony. He was the Wagner conductor par excellence at the Metropolitan, conducting many operas without a score. He ended his career as the professor of conducting at the Juilliard School of Music. He was called a conductor's conductor.

Then right there, in a bare waiting room in Newfoundland, he turned to me and said for all to hear, "This one's for you Lasse." And then started to play Povel Ramel's hit Johanssons Boogie Woogie Waltz. It was also sort of an acknowledgement from Sixten, who had shared many pleasant evenings with my father at the Operakällaren restaurant when they were both finished for the evening, he at the opera and my father at the Oscars Theater.

Here at Gander after the lean years in London and the not yet recovered Sweden, I had my first overwhelming encounter with an American Banana Split.

I had a lot to learn in America. One of the first was to pull up my pants to half-mast. I found that all American businessmen had the pants flagging around the ankles. I also had to buy a pair of clumsy shoes instead of the stylish Italians I was wearing, as I believe the Americans felt they were a bit feminine. Not to mention short sleeved white shirts and color crazy ties. My discreet British ties and Irish Linen cuff linked shirts sort of came to feel snobbish. They all came to fit in better weeks later in Hollywood.

Ford Motor Company's international PR office was in Manhattan. My first impression here was how clean and fresh everyone was. All the men in white, albeit short sleeved white shirts and all the females seemed fresh as spring. In Sweden at Ford the men wore the same shirt for a week. Deodorant was unknown. And in the secretary pool you could always feel that someone had her period.

I was so impressed with all the clean white shirts, the morning fresh female dresses - if you know what I mean - that I decided to put it in my first PR report back home to Stockholm.

Those familiar with Swedish offices during the 1940's and 50's recall when opening the front door provided ventilation. Know what I mean? To this day we have not fully caught up with the American habit of a clean white shirt every day and the air in a secretary pool scented of newly cut flowers.

My second culinary experience, after the banana split at Gander, was my first American steak. I hardly believed my eyes when I saw the T- bone on my plate at Jack Dempsey's restaurant on Broadway. The steaks seem smaller today, but in the 50's there seemed to be steak frenzy. Maybe you understand my amazement after horsemeat in London and tough Swedish beef from cows that died of old age. And the flavor!

Henry Ford II had been to Stockholm on a short visit. (Yes. his pants also flagged at half-mast). I had taken some small part in celebrating his visit. In Dearborn as a result I was given a spectacular guidance around the River Rouge Plant. At the main office, high up among the executive suites, all the old men looked the same. They could have changed faces without it making much difference. I bet it was not any different at General Motors. I had a generous allowance of $25 a day. After spending some time with the PR people in Dearborn I applied to Stockholm for time to allow me to see a bit more of America.

I started by taking a Greyhound bus to Miami lured by the land of oranges and the fact that after 42nd Street in New York, the best jazz in America was played on Second Avenue in Miami and Frank Sinatra sang at Everglades Hotel and the whole city was swinging - years before Miami Beach was broken in, so to say.

On the island the first hotels were being built art deco style. Up to 30th Street rich Jews from New York and Mafia families mostly occupied them. As the Beach caught on nationally, the hotels became bigger and bigger. Already in 1956 the Fontainebleau Hilton on 56th street was the world's largest beach hotel. The hotels towards the bottom end of the island slipped back into rooming for old people, mostly Jews from New York. South Beach was like a mile long porch of old people in rocking chairs paying $30 a month for a room with hot plate, and picking thrown out stale bread from behind the super market.

South Beach, or SoBe, is the world's largest old folk home turned into the world's most fashionable place to strut your stuff and show the size of God's gifts to you.

Miami Beach became a place full of gangsters in residence, which in turn made it one of the safest places in America. It was the only place where the mafia families and gangsters like Al Capone could live in peace. It was out of bounds for killings.

Miami Beach grew rapidly to the north past 100th street. North of several blocks of big hotels and hi rise condos opened a row of beach motels, many carrying names that, if you were familiar with the Mafia's many places in Las Vegas you would recognize the owners - Desert Inn, The Sahara, The Sands, The Dunes, etc.

The Mafia families loosened up a bit twenty years later when North Miami Beach hit borders with the city of Hallandale. Even today you read about drive by shootings in this city that was founded by the preacher Bengt Magnus Johansson from the village of Drängsered in the district of Halland in Sweden. He took the name Halland when he started work as a preacher in Michigan. Bad health made him move to the sun in Florida where he built a small congregation and on a hill about fifteen miles north of Miami he built his church and called the place Hallandale. 150,000 people live in that city today.

In Stockholm I had met a lady friend of Gustav Wally (a member of the Swedish finance family Wallenberg) who took the modern musicals to Sweden after an unsuccessful career in Hollywood as a new Fred Astair. He was just too tall, about 6'5 and not a gifted enough dancer. And he was gay which was one hell of a sin in those days. Anyway, he informed her of my wish to see Hollywood. So one day I jumped on a DC3, hopped from one airport to another, until I arrived in Los Angeles.

A driver met me at the airport and asked me if I had a tuxedo. What the heck should I have a tuxedo for?

"Because," the driver said, "the Mrs. has a big party for you tonight.

She had made a lot of friends visiting Sweden and had fallen in love with the Dalecarlia type of farm court, a so-called Dalagård. She had copied one as her residence in Malibu, which was then called the Malibu Movie Colony. She had an opening night with a bunch of Hollywood's biggest stars. My role was to play the part of the guy who had flown in from Sweden for just this occasion. I remember Gary Cooper was there and so was Claudette Colbert.

And the stay there? It can be hard work not to get up 'til about noon, revive with a dip in the pool and then have a pm cocktail at the bar before putting on the rented tuxedo for dining and nightclubbing. For me to see a private swimming pool was as sensational as for a Russian soldier to see a water closet.

The only swimming pools we had in Sweden were at a couple of bath houses: Sportpalatset, Centralbadet where the school children learned to swim and Stur-

ebadet where people like my father used to go in the mornings for a sauna, a dip in the pool and breakfast. He brought an American friend with him one day who rushed back to the dressing room and put on long johns when he saw that the scrubbers were women.
"Can I understand from this," he asked my father, " that you have male scrubbers for the ladies?"

The visit to LA gave me an opportunity to see an old friend, Alf Kjellin from the days we shared a table at a food service "matservering" in Hedemora, Dalecarlia, during the filming of the Bergman scripted Frenzy ('Hets'). Alf had been recruited by MGM I think it was, as someone they felt could become a new Robert Taylor. Alf tried out in minor roles in a couple of films and did not like it. He felt better behind the camera and became one of Hollywood's foremost directors of TV series. Most of Streets of San Francisco and Hawaii 5 0 were directed by him. He was known for being "on budget, on time."

Alf lived high up on Mulholland Drive in Beverly Hills where you could see Los Angeles below when the gas smoggy layer did not obstruct the view. He used to say that on a clear day you could see Los Angeles - a day when the breeze from the ocean chased the smog into the mountains or out to sea.

Alf's home was a meeting place for so many of Hollywood's Swedes such as Signe Hasso, Viveka Lindfors, Bibi Andersson, Max von Sydow, and Ingrid Bergman etc. People just liked Alf Kjellin. But it was not only the famous who loved him. Born in 1920, he took as his task in life helping refugee children and never seemed to have less than a dozen living in the house. He got up every morning at four or five to make sure they had breakfast before he left for work at six. He left behind a large number of parent- less children for whom he had opened his home.

As a Swede, I was not used to meeting many unmarried multi millionaires, I was not very familiar with their feelings, habits and lifestyle. The Queen of Oranges, as all called her, suddenly decided to live in New York City for a while and to sell the place in Malibu. She started to sell out inventories and she called on me at Alf's place and wondered if I wanted to buy that 12 cylinder Lincoln Continental Convertible that I had admired so much. I could have it, she said, for a thousand dollars and pay her from Sweden when I got home. She said that she had bought it from Judy Garland. I had to drive it to New York and when thinking about that I made a big mistake. I asked if she would come with me. Have you ever tried to put a millionnairess in a $3 motel room or eat at diners!!? Thought not!

I figured that with gas at 25 cents a gallon, motels for three to four dollars a night and sparse eating, I should be able to make it to New York. But I had of course not calculated with the Queen of Oranges. Neither had I calculated with the fact that the locomotive heavy Lincoln was a gas-guzzling devil. Still, I had some traveler's checks in reserve.

We plowed through the Mojave Desert and the Petrified Forest. Then suddenly the twelve-cylinder engine gave up on a couple of them. We found a garage in a God forsaken place called Albuquerque in New Mexico. The Lady was now markedly irritated. I remarked that she should have checked these plugs a long time ago.

"Spark plugs, what the %^@! are you talking about?" she said as if it was my fault that the engine misfired on half of the cylinders.

By St. Louis I had used up all my cash so I suggested we should stay over night at a hotel so that I could go to a bank in the morning.

"What are you supposed to do at the bank?"

"Cash some travelers checks".

"Travelers checks?! In St Louis?! In Missouri?! They

wouldn't even know what you are talking about!"

She was right. The men at the bank just looked at the checks, held them against the light and called in some guys from the back rooms that inspected them, thumbed them and then looked at each other.

It was as if they felt these checks either came from outer space or that I had printed them myself.

I asked the lady if she happened to have any money and she replied something about a lady traveling with a gentleman had no need to bring any money. The next morning I went to a pawnbroker with my gold watch.

Would the person who bought an 18 carat gold wrist watch with the inscription LHO about 60 years ago, please contact the writer!!

I learned a few things in America on that first trip. Don't lend money to colleagues who like to show you the town - as in Miami. And don't drive cross-country with ladies who don't like to eat at diners.

What happened to the Lincoln? It arrived in Stockholm. There was only one other like it. Financier Max Gumpel who used to drive his friend Greta Garbo in it when she was in town owned it.

I had to sell it.

Parked in my spot in the executive garage at Ford, Otto Brøndum called the guard and asked,

"Whose car is that and why is it in here? Get it out!"

"It's the PR manager's car, sir".

"I don't care if it is the king's. Get rid of it!"

I learned from this that if your boss is president of an automobile producing company you'd better not outshine him by driving a finer car than he drives. And honestly, my wife was not very fond of it either. She said she felt embarrassed to be seen in a car that was nothing but a 'skrytbubbla' (a bragging piece). I sold it with a heavy heart to an executive at an advertising agency.

I thought I had forgotten all about this tragic love affair when ten years later I found it parked in my parking space in Skönstaholm. It had been converted into a V8 hot rod street racer and what we call a 'raggarbil' in Sweden.

I patted my old friend and said: "We all experience changes in life, don't we?" And it was as if he had answered "Like you with your Malibu friend."

Ten years later, this model Lincoln having become a collector's item sold at an auction in California for $125,000. There were only a couple of hundred made when the war stopped production.

Otto Brøndum was a man of many moods. He was short on explanations. When the advertising budget was cut but the goals set higher, he met the complaint with, "This just makes it a tad bit more difficult, doesn't it?" When I asked for a company car for trips to printers, agencies etc, he was in a negative mood and told me no.

"So how and what do I do?"

"That's your business," he said,

I called a friend at Volkswagen and asked if he could lend me a car. He was delighted to do so.

I made sure I parked as close to Brøndum as possible in the garage.

"Who the hell is driving a Volkswagen here?" He called out very upset.

"The PR Manager, sir," said the guard.

Called into his office I expected to be raked over the coals, if not fired. But he just looked up and handed me an approved request for a company car.

"But..." I sort of stammered.

He looked up and said that he knew what he had told me and then added,

"Young man, you showed gutsy initiative".

One of my jobs, aside from creating advertising campaigns, arranging company events and managing an ice racing team in the winter was to get prominent persons to drive a Ford. Every year we changed Prince Bertil's Lincoln for a new one. It was quite a ceremony at the prince's villa on Djurgården. It helped of course publicity wise as he was known as the Motor Prince'.

Anna Lisa Eriksson was one of the most popular comediennes in Sweden and a close friend of mine since childhood when she had often stayed with us. One day she called and asked me to go with her to meet some Italian producers, Ponti and Soldati, at Grand Hotel. They were in Sweden to find a new young female face, a bit boyish, for a pirate movie.

It proved soon that Anna Lisa was not the type. So I asked them about how they had conducted their search so far. It seemed they had just done the routine of the drama and film schools. I suggested that they should also try some of the photo studios doing commercial work. We ended up at the Uggla Studio at Kungsgatan. Suddenly a girl passed from one end of the room to the other on her way to the dark room.

"That's her!" Shouted Ponti.

The poor girl did not have a clue what it was all about and seemed scared when they turned her around and examined her assets. I tried to explain it but it was hard. Anyway, she finally agreed to come to the film studio at Filmstaden in Råsunda the next morning at nine for a screen test. I doubted she would turn up because she had seemed so scared. But at nine she was there. Then, apparently frightened by all the commotion - camera men, sound mixers, light setters and a dozen more on the floor, when it was time for a test she was gone.

"Find her and bring her back," shouted Ponti at me. I had difficulties in understanding what they saw in this perfectly common looking Swedish girl. But of course, I was no filmmaker.

I had a picture of her and knew she lived on the suburban island of Lidingö but neither the studio nor I had an address. So I got in my car and drove to Lidingö. I went from street to street, showed the photo and asked people if they knew her. After an hour or so a couple of boys said,

"That's May Britt! She lives in the brown villa at the end of the street."

It was a two-story house with two apartments.

The mother opened the door. I did not feel very welcome. Maybritt ran into her room and closed the door.

"The girl does not want to. And who knows what kind those men are!"

I did not have much experience in trying to talk young girls into becoming film stars, and if the father had not come home from work at that time, I might have given up trying. He was a mailman, a calm and steady working class Swede.

"Hey darling, what have you got to lose? Mother will be with you. Lars says his wife will be there too; making sure it's safe all around. And you hear Lars telling you that if you don't like it or can't handle it after a couple of weeks you can come back home".

About five o'clock I had the girl back in the studio. The test turned out great. Ponti was pleased and so was Soldati who always agreed with Ponti. Yes, the Ponti married to Sophia Loren.

"Get the girl some clothes and make sure she's in Rome in two weeks".

My wife spent a couple of days shopping with May Britt at Nordiska Kompaniet, NK in Stockholm. She had never had any "real clothes."

After a couple of days in Rome she disappeared into the world of Cinecittà and from our horizon. The mother stayed with her for a while and we understood that she had signed a contract for several films. The first that caused the search was about a girl who, disguised as a boy, joins the crew of a pirate ship.

Most Europeans who made movies at Cinecittà film studios in Rome sooner or later surfaced in Hollywood. May Britt was no exception. She never reached any stardom or even close to it. But she met Sammy Davis Jr. and caused a racial scandal when she married him. During a time when mixed marriages were scorned, May Britt suffered humiliating treatment by crowds that turned up demonstrating outside wherever she stayed with Sammy. I think that it was the Rat Pack with Frank Sinatra as primus who took Sammy and her into their artistic embrace that helped her stay with Sammy for so long. Now and then, late at night you might find a movie called The Rat Pack on TV.

While she was still married to Sammy she came to Sweden with him for a show in Stockholm. There was a reception at Operakällaren afterwards. I went up to her and said ""Hi, May Britt." She looked at me and I felt that perhaps as my hair had grown white she might not recognize me.

"I am Lars Henrik Ottoson, remember?"

"No I don't."

I just stood there feeling like an idiot when there was a hand on my shoulder and someone said,

"They get big headed and forgetful in Hollywood, don't they?"

It was her father, the mailman.

I believe May Britt still lives in Beverly Hills or thereabout and that she is fairly well off, One who knows her is Barbro Klint, my one time fabulous secretary for many joyous years in Stockholm. She nourished an American dream and one day she left me and took off for New York. I finally found her thanks to SWEA, in Beverly Hills where she had a travel agency.

May Britt makes me think of another more successful but tragic Swedish star in Hollywood - my goddaughter of sorts, Inger Stevens.

It all started in 1940 at the 'Familjebidragsnämnden,' the Swedish Family Allowance Center. My wife Lill worked there and she shared a desk with a divorced young woman, Lisbeth Stensland, who liked to go dancing on Saturday nights. Lill and I were still looking for a place of our own. When Lisbeth was out swinging to Seymor Österwall's Orchestra at Royal on Drottninggatan or with Topsy Lindblom at Nalen, we were happy to baby-sit little Inger. The father had disappeared to America. At the end of the war he wanted his daughter to come and live with him in Chicago. I think Lisbeth was perfectly happy to send her off.

From Chicago the father took a job in Los Angeles. Inger was growing into a beautiful teenager who took dance lessons. How Ingrid Stensland came to be Inger Stevens on a fast track to the very top in a Hollywood that saw her as a new Lana Turner. She had looks and talent. She was paired with actors like Gary Cooper, Glen Ford, and James Stewart. She starred with Clint Eastwood in Hang'em High.

She had a rather complicated love life. She had affaires with most of her leading men and kept the dark secret that she was married almost since her teens to a black football player, Ike Jones. They lived apart. She was the star in the enormously popular TV series The Farmer's Daughter. In 1970 she was to marry Burt Reynolds. A couple of weeks before the marriage she was found dying on the bathroom floor of her home in Hollywood Hills by her maid. It was written off as a suicide from sleeping pills washed down with alcohol. But was it really suicide? Or was it yet another case of Hollywood cover up? Her face had traces of knife wounds covered with a fresh bandage.

Another female star in Burt Reynolds love life, Sarah Miles, found her husband dead when she returned from

Burt Reynolds hotel room at 3 am. Police Sergeant Forest Hinderliter, who handled the Inger Stevens case says:
 "I said it was murder then. I say it is murder today."

From Cape to Cape—a trip of 36,000 miles through 34 countries, using 20,000 gallons of gasoline and 100 gallons of oil while wearing out six tires with four half worn.

FROM CAPE TO CAPE

There were situations in life that caused even my widely recognized patience to ebb. Or burn up. Whatever. It happened one day in December of 1952 during an executive staff meeting at Ford.

My predecessor at the company, Claes Livijn had left his post at Junex and returned to Ford due to his old friendship with Otto Brøndum. He had no defined function in the sales section and had tried for weeks to nab a piece here and a piece there and as much as he could from my section. I.e. me...

This very special day he said:

"I have, as you know, been advertising manager here for sixteen years before Lars Henrik so maybe if you listen to me about this...."

That's when I blew up and said:

"You have been advertising manager here for sixteen years; you may damn well be it for another sixteen!"

Having said that, I left the room called for a taxi and left the building.

It was stupid of course, but that guy had been on my nerves for months and I guess I am not much of a fall in line corporation man.

However, I turned the mistake into a success. Had to.

Otto Brøndum called me at home. A bit sourly, but still friendly enough, he wondered what my plans were now. I told him that he would know fairly soon. Two weeks later on the front page of the large daily Stockholms-Tidningen he would find a four-column headline over a photo of me in front of a Volkswagen Bus. The text began:

> The head of Ford Motor Company's PR section in Sweden, Lars Henrik Ottoson, is about to drive a Volkswagen on a record trip from North Cape in Norway to Cape Town in South Africa, the longest overland drive ever attempted.

I had to do something drastic because the way I left Ford did not, I realized, make me very attractive to other corporations. I needed to do something that made people understand that I left for something adventurous and different.

No one had ever taken a car from the northernmost tip of Europe to the southernmost tip of Africa. Mainly because it had been regarded as much too dangerous. And there was also the practical reason that the roads up north in ice country and the desert stretches in the Sahara were never open at the same time of year.

Volkswagen's head office in Germany thought it was a tremendous idea and told Swedish Volkswagen to supply a well-equipped car. VW in Germany also wanted a 16 mm documentary from the trip. ESSO contributed enough cash to pay for the gas even if we had to buy it from other sources. Then I was able to secure a large advance from the publishing company Gebers. Something else played into my hands. The Royal Swedish Automobile Club (KAK) was celebrating its 50th anniversary and decided to name the tour its Fifty Years Jubilee Drive. On the strength of that I received a special introductory letter from the Swedish Prime Minister Tage Erlander.

The only thing missing was a co-driver/photographer willing to come along for the adventure and share in the possible profits afterwards. Bengt Lindström worked for a photo studio in Stockholm. He was five years my junior, played soccer for Westermalm and was called Kritan. However, he could not come along right away because he had to get his papers and passport in order and a driver's license. While he worked on getting all that in order, I was lucky to get a recognized press photographer Roland Palm to come with me up to North Cape for the drive down to Stockholm. (We experienced several adventures through later years.)

We drove to Trondheim, Norway and shipped to Hammerfest, called the world's northernmost city. From there we ferried over to Honningsvåg and drove up to Magerøya to photograph the VW with its front looking over the ice towards the North Pole.

Turning the van to the south the big trip began. In Hammerfest we discussed the road conditions with customs inspector Birger Hansen at a time when nature did its best up there to get rid of people. The sea had just taken a couple from a harbor street and an avalanche half buried seven children playing only fifty feet from the Town Hall.

"Yes, it may be beautiful here with sea and mountains meeting, but it is hard," said Hansen. "Hell knows if you can get through Finnmarksvidda 'cause there is no road open until May. It might be beautiful up here but it is rough living. In the autumn you can hardly walk because of the storms. In the winter you can't get through anywhere because of the snow. In the spring you wade in mud over your ankles. And the summer is so short that you hardly notice it".

"It's real bad", said Mrs. Hansen. "Savagely bad."

"She has difficulties adjusting," said Hansen. " She is from Tromsø and used to more big city like conditions." Tromsø is a port further north than 'Treriksröset,' the northern point of Sweden.

The road, or whatever one could call it, began at the end of the fjord of Porsanger and to get there we had to take the ferry. When the ship signaled cast off down in the fishing harbor the place was full of waving locals. Mothers held up their small children so they could get a glimpse of the crazy Swedes.

We had left the world's northernmost town with mayor Ørjan Østvik's signature and endorsement on top of the KAK roll and we had just started to collect latitudes. Ahead of us, the snow seemed packed to mountain heights. Cut through the snow was a two-meter wide strip of road with snow around it so deep that the top of the van could not be seen above it. We also had to remove the side view mirrors.

The road ended at Laukavann just as Hansen had predicted. It ended outside the old mountain man Ole Grotte's cabin. We went inside to ask if he knew about a tractor we had ordered for pulling us across the snow land to where the road could be picked up again. Grotte told us that the tractor got stuck further up with a broken oil pipe. The driver, Einar Jensen had skied to the village of Karasjok to get the pipe welded. So we just housed ourselves on Grotte's kitchen floor in front of the wood stove on which a pot of coffee greeted any and every visitor. The furnishings in the cabin's only room consisted of a crude table, a wicker chair, and a bed with a set of drawers and a second wicker chair with three legs. Nevertheless, in this godforsaken land of snow Grotte was a big man because he had a telephone. He was already eighty years old when he rebuilt the cabin after the war.

We slept on the floor as the winds from outside fed us with a floor draft in all musical keys.

Now and then some Lapp came in, changed the hay in his boots ('skallor'), grabbed a mug of coffee and went back outside in the dark. One Lapp looked at my double bottomed, special leather climber's boots and said they looked like nice summer shoes.

As a Lapp took his hay out of his boots, he spread it on the floor by the stove to dry. He then poured a mug of coffee, acid as hell, and sat down to pick the marrow from a reindeer bone. The air in the kitchen was fortified by the odor of snuff spit hitting the stove.

The third morning Einar Jensen arrived with his seven-ton band tractor and an eight-meter long loading sled.

The last we saw of Grotte was his keg waving in the air as his liquor was still burning in our throats. Grotte had never been much for percentage when it came to his liquor. Then he went back to the cabin he said he would paint in the summer

Three kilometers from Laukavann, in the midst of the Finnvidda plateau, the diesel engine started spluttering. The oil pipe had broken again. If we had known... Anyway Jensen put on his skis, took the pipe and set off for Karasjok. He could not make it back before dark. Maybe tomorrow afternoon.

Roland and I looked at each other and sort of said, "Who eats first?" We had dry food for a couple of days and coffee. The wind was hauling; the van was shaking but was too secured at the tractor set to fall over. We got into our sleeping bags in the back. We couldn't run the engine for heat, as we did not know how far we had to drive before we hit a gas station. Instead we fired up our Primus stove and put a brick on top. A Lapp skied by. He stopped and looked at us for a moment, then disappeared among the snow dunes. A pack of wolves came right up to us, sniffing around. We scared them off with the horn. The next day just before noon, the Lapp came back. Again, he stopped for a moment looking at us. When I rolled down the window he looked into the van and said, "God damn cold, isn't it?" and skied on.

The tractor broke down again twice and it took us another seventeen hours to reach Karasjok, just about ten miles away, where we found food and showers and an open road ahead. It was just that we also had to pass Tana River where they just had taken down the wooden bridge in anticipation of the spring flood. Once the bridge was down the road would be closed for weeks. It took over twenty years before a permanent bridge was built. So there we were, Roland and I, at sunset without a clue about how to get across.

Suddenly they were there. Finns and Norwegians... about twenty of them. They started to clear a path through the snow down to the river. Then they put planks on the still frozen river to distribute the weight over a larger surface.

"You can try now," said one of the men, believing that the ice would hold.

It did, but there were some anxious minutes when we heard the ice crack as we passed over it with water up to the axels.

Here in northern Finland, you help each other. On the other side of the river we stopped to thank our helpers. There were none of them to be seen. In the lands of the Lapps, in Sweden, Norway and Finland, where they herd across the borders, there is no time for thank you and small talk. You just help each other and make no big deal of it.

Now we had only two hard days drive to Haparanda, the northernmost city along the Baltic coastline in Sweden. The distances up there are big. Further south, somewhere south of Örnsköldsvik, Roland took a turn at the wheel. I stretched out in the back and went to sleep. Suddenly I was thrown out of the bunk as the car rolled over. I felt some pain in my head and traced carefully with my hand. It got wet. I did not even dare to look at it. Oh my God, blood, I thought. I just shut my eyes fearing the adventure was over before it started. I finally dared to look at my hand. It was not blood. It was buttermilk!

Roland had fallen asleep and skidded off the icy road into the ditch, where, thank God, the deep snow softened the fall onto the side causing very little damage. Hallelujah the bus was whole but I had it checked out at the VW factory shop in Södertälje to make sure.
When we arrived in Stockholm, Bengt Lindström took Roland Palm's place.

The trip did not turn out to be just an adventure. It also allowed us to meet and come to know many individuals, adventurers, reality escapers and different souls. We met the first in Saltsjöbaden before we left Stockholm. His name was Leo Komstedt. His rich Pentecostal father had just made him sell his film company Iris Film, because movies were a deadly sin. To save his inheritance Leo sold out and nourished wild dreams about an expedition to Kalahari in South Africa to find the quagga, a miniature horse animal that was extinct except in Leo's mind. Now he spent his time in the basement of his house in Saltsjöbaden where he had arranged a shooting range. He experimented with different kinds of ammunition and mixed his own powder for different types of rifles. He also tested the camera market's four best sellers with every film type available. He photographed one and the same vase over and over with the same speed setting and the same timing, and then compared the negatives. He was determined to have only the best before heading south to find the quagga.

We met him later in Tangier, where he had a house on the hill above the Kasbah, as Bengt and I had to do a detour to Volkswagen's head office and factory in Germany. We then drove as fast as we could through Europe until we hit the Spanish border, where our richly equipped van shook up the Spanish customs guys.

"Bienvenuti a Espania," I tried pointing to the happy faces on the tourist posters. "La siento mucho senor," said the customs guy politely. But meant of course, you are kidding.

We paid roundly to drive into a Spain that only five years before had shed the middle ages for the twentieth century.

Avoiding the temptation to buy beach land for $100 an acre as we conquered the beat up gravel road along the Spanish southern Riviera, we caught a ferry in Torremolinos crossing the Strait of Gibraltar to Tangier.

Tanger, or Tangier, in the 1950's was an independent tax heaven and black money capital. There were over 400 banks, some not more than a hole in the wall, but still functioning banks. With its touristy Kasbah, its elegant boulevards and exclusive cafes, this was a mini country - administered by Morocco. No one asked from where you came or how you made your millions. In name, Tangier belonged to the Sultan of Morocco but was governed by his nebdoub plus a board consisting of six muslims, four Spaniards, four Frenchmen, three Brits, three Americans and one Italian, one Belgian one Dutchman and one Portuguese.

Tangier remained one of the most remarkable political soups ever concocted well into the sixties. But there were those who meant that Tangier was important as a place to embrace stateless and political refugees. The only professions for which you needed a license were doctors and attorneys. And no one, not even the banks, were required to keep any books.

In this mini country that was governed by thirty assembly members of eleven nationalities, the official languages were French, Spanish and Arabic. Tangier had four post offices - a Spanish, a French, a British and Arabic. The mail from abroad came to the post office that the mail-carrying airline cared to leave it to. So all you had to do was visit four post offices to check your mail. There were no mail carriers.

Leo's white, villa at the top of the hill overlooking the town, was in a rich area of wide avenues, luxury boutiques and fine houses. Everything was breathing respectability, which, if you considered the people who lived there, was rather grotesque. Tangier above the Kasbah was a place where some of the biggest crooks in the world became the most respected moral snobs. In that part of town with no visible sins, no nightclubs were allowed and shame did not wear spike heels.

You could sit on Leo's roof terrace and see the lights of the city and the ships passing through the Strait of Gibraltar. The sight came accompanied by the monotonous rambling of the Arab guard Mustafa and his woman. He never left the house because Allah had shown him a fine hut to live in with water and electric light and even paid him to live there. The only thing he had to do was to sit outside the garage door and see to it that no strangers entered the yard.

The Swedish consulate in Tangier was, for some unexplainable reason, in the Kasbah next to a society brothel called The Black Cat. We had drinks there a couple of times. More than that, we could not afford. The Madam was a formidable big sized female. She looked as if she weighed two hundred kilos of which she put about a third on the bar counter to relieve her feet. She complained about the times.

"The tourists seem to have less money than before," she said. "All these group tours are no good for the girls and the new chief of police has stopped me from showing some beautiful sex movies. What is the world coming to? I miss the old police chief. He was such a gentleman and came in at least a couple of times a month to watch the new films. Yes, such a gentleman," she reminisced.

To get out of Tangier we needed an exit visa with two signatures. To get it took two days. Everything took time in public offices where Muslims, Christians and Jews created three holidays a week to show religious respect for each other. Then of course you add Sunday. Once we had our visa we received an armed escort to the border of Spanish Morocco. It was not to protect us but to make sure that we did not lose some shooting iron on the way.

The road from Tangier led through a nationalistic Arab world brimming of desire to end the French sovereignty in Algeria. The heat had been welling in from the Sahara earlier than expected. In one week, the desert winds had killed off most plants and flowers. It was hot and dusty on the roads and everything suggested that it would be better to drive during the cooler night hours - except the French border officer. He did not think so because of the Arabian insurgents.

"But," I said, "All tourist reports mention how safe it is all along the coastal road to Algiers."

"Monsieur, it is never safe around here."

"You mean to say that there are risks of attacks?"

"Not exactly great, not exactly small, but a lonely car is always a temptation."

We had about eighty kilometers over the Zegotta pass and reckoned that it would take about two hours. The sun was about to set and in spite of the warning we took off into the dark.

After a sharp left turn up in the mountains, a truck almost blocked the road. Two Arabs waved to us to stop. The border guard's advice rang in my ears: "drive on, don't stop."

I stopped and immediately put the gear in reverse and backed away some fifty meters and then, fast from first to second gear, floored the accelerator and passed the narrow gap with a roar.

The Arabs jumped into the ditch as a stone crashed our rear window. Bengt took out our Husqvarna rifle. We watched the truck taking off after us. Should we be able to outrun it? Yes, as long as the ten kilometers ahead to the village of Lonelja was full of curbs, switchbacks and downhill. On a straight road or uphill we would not have a chance against the truck. We were doing sixty mph downhill and through the curves with our equipment rolling all over the place in the back.

We made it and reaching the Prefect's office, we parked as the Arabs drove by fisting us.

We were heading for Fez, Rue du Train 7, across the street from the barracks of the Foreign Legion.

A threatening German shepherd greeted us before Madam Malleray appeared and invited us in. She was a young, slim-trim good-looking woman, who actually looked more like a Swedish parson's wife than the wife of one of the toughest and most decorated soldiers in the Foreign Legion, Captain Jean de Malleray. Fourteen years as a Legionnaire's wife in North Africa and the Far East had still not totally erased the Swedishness in the daughter of Anne Mari Johansson and her taxicab-owning husband. We told her about our little adventure in the mountains.

"If Jean had been with you, he would have stopped. He likes things like that," she said.

She said that more in passing. When we asked where he was now, she said he had been four years in Indo China because, "he likes it out there, and a real Legionnaire does that."

"And the true wife of a Legionnaire accepts that?"

"Of course, and she is proud of it," said Anne Mari."

The world is full of weaklings and it's wonderful to know that you are not married to one of them but to a real MAN. I visit him out there and he comes home for a couple of weeks twice a year."

"All that you hear about the Legion," explained Anne Mari, "is mostly stories from hell painting deserters. Of course it's tough in the Legion. Maybe tougher than in any other military unit, but that has to do with the kind of soldier material you have to work with. We are making soldiers out of no-gooders and scum from across the world. The Legion is often their last chance to live a productive life outside of prison walls. For so many of them it means a fresh new start in life. The Legion needs all kinds of people - engineers, doctors, photographers, office staff... you name it. Look at Jean. He joined as a soldier and he is a captain now. He brings milk and food to villages. He takes sick natives to the dispensary. He is a soft hearted professional soldier, more a protector than an aggressor."

When the Gothic style triumphed in Europe, the powerful sultans of the Meridin family created a wondrous town in the valley of Sebous. Their nation covered the whole of North Africa and Andalusia. On the most beautiful hill above Fez, they built a mausoleum. From there, their forefathers could look out over the walls and minarets of the capital, and far away, the snow clad heights of the Atlas Mountains. Already, seven hundred years ago, two hundred thousand Moroccans lived inside the walls of this city that still stands as one of the mightiest in the Old World. We looked out over the city from one of the olive hills. Anne Mari told us it was the most beautiful sight in Morocco. The first sun beams were waking the thousand year old medina quarters and played their shimmering game in the golden globes of the mosques and played a light game on the walls. It looked like the glittering of a water clear diamond on a dark green velvety cloth. I have returned to Fez many times. This extraordinary place seems to always be calling to you. In the old part of the city, Fes el Bali or Fes Medina, the time seems to have stood still for hundreds of years. The streets are too narrow for anything but pack mules. We parked outside the Kasbah in the Fes Medina where, according to the French reporters, the Tharaud brothers, everything is as old as Herod and as full of lice as Job.

To walk through the medina in Fez was like walking in a world where time had stood still. The streets were like cracks between the houses and if you stretched your arms out you could rest your hands on both walls. There were the carpet merchants and the silversmiths, pack animals, and water sellers and dirt, which only occasional rains could wash away. It was like walking through a timeless abstraction. Tharaud said about the Moroccan that he is not inclined to find something new and therefore everything he builds today looks exactly like what he built yesterday.

The hot wind unleashed itself on us as we drove east through Morocco into Algeria. Still, it was pretty tepid compared to what hit us later.

Instead of hooking up to the trans Saharan route in Colomb Beachar, we had to drive to Algiers to get a permit allowing us to cross the desert that was closed to all motor traffic this time of the year. It was too hot in the desert even for the Foreign Legion that withdrew its units in May because of the heat. We had to apply for a special permit from Le Service des Affaires Sahariennes, Direction des Territoires du Sud. It was not a welcome application because the bureau did not want to send out people and then have to mount a costly expedition to save them or to just pick up the bodies. Big truck convoys did the only crossing of the desert once a month. We could not sit around and wait but wouldn't have had a choice if it had not been for the Swedish consul in Algiers, René Kohler. He was so well connected we received one of those unique permits.

He simply said it was such an honor to be the Swedish Honorary Consul that he was pleased to have been able to help us.

Now, was this really such a big affair crossing the desert alone and off-season?

An association called Association des Amies du Sahara, based in Paris, recorded every off-season individual crossing since 1924. I have a plaque numbered 126.

We used the time in Algiers to go through our equipment and consult with old desert foxes that all thought we were in something a bit over our heads. We bought twenty jerry cans for water and gas and fifty liters of oil, twenty-one cans of food, and a kerosene lamp.

We also played tourists a bit in the city and took walks in the Kasbah to relive where Jean Gabin in and as Pépé le Moko, had escaped over the roofs. And where a lovesick Charles Boyer, in the American version, Pepe from Marseille, ran after Hedy Lamarr through the narrow alleys. But most of the time we sat at one or the other of the cafes on Rue Charles Peny and looked at the fair Algerian girls.

A tall, thin, strange looking figure with a knotty red beard wearing a striped T-shirt, knee long shorts, of the kind that are modern today, but were not then, and short suede boots of the Kenya model, came up to us.

"Are you Mr. Ottoson? My name is Ian Mitchie and I have chased you all over town. I have heard that you are about to cross the desert, and you are my last chance."

"Fat chance," I said.

We were already so over loaded that I was considering sending some equipment by ship to Nigeria.

Somewhere out there in the desert, in the sands of Tanezrouft, his pal watched over a car with a broken back axle at a small military post due to be closed and evacuated. His friend had been sitting there for a couple of weeks. Of course he had no permit to cross the desert because he came from the south where there was no controlling authority.

"Please," he said, "it's hotter than hell for my friend out there and he'll be short of everything when the military leaves. Then, if he is forced to leave the car we lose everything we worked three years for in Tanganyika. I don't have a penny left and to get here I paid Arab truck drivers almost as much as it costs to fly to America."

The next morning, much against our better sense, we packed him and his axle in the back, and drove with kneeing rear wheels towards Colomb Bechar on roads that looked like corrugated roofs. I soon realized that with this load, the VW could not handle more of the rough roads. Just as we left the fertile fruit belt heading inland, I drove off the road and cruised on the hard ground of thorn bushes rather than wait for shock absorbers and springs to fail. Flat tires were easier to fix than broken parts.

We made camp the first night outside a small god forgotten place called Mecheria. It was Bengt's job to pick the thorns from the tires, maintain the air pressure at two thirds to leave a margin for pressure increase during the heat of the day when the ground was hot as a frying pan, and check the gas and oil.

Suddenly Bengt cried out. A scorpion that had been waiting for him behind the front wheel had stung him. I said Mecheria was a god-forsaken place - with a small military post and a nursing station. We were there within twenty minutes and Bengt was already in bad shape. Luckily it was a yellow scorpion. A black one would have been worse than a rattlesnake's bite. Bengt would have a couple of days with high fever, which was an inconvenience we had to reckon with, so we decided to camp right there. At the dispensary, a nurse said, " welcome to Mecheria, the Scorpion Capital of the World." And that was not a joke. At the military post, the commandant paid five francs for every captured scorpion. In May alone, they caught over 4,000!

If it had not been for Bengt, we would not have stopped at the Foreign Legion base, Beni Ounif, to have the military doctor give him an injection. We spent a day at the Hotel Trans Saharienne drinking cold beer at the bar. The host just threw us the bottles and can opener. Then he spit brown tobacco on the floor. He did not like guests, we soon found out. At least not the kind of guests that frequented his place.

A Legionnaire who stood at the counter remarked,

"Sometimes I think that the Legion has put this guy here for us to feel at home. The Legion is a sheer hell messieurs."

"Is it that hard?"

"It is not the physical harshness. Most of us can handle that. It is the loneliness and monotony and resentment by locals. Of course, some like it more than others, like the two over there in the corner. Many turn gay in the Legion. The other day, I had to beat up two fags who tried to engage me and now I am being isolated. But some times I wonder if it was worth it, because the two guys over there are obviously happier than I am. Those two on the sofa at least have something to do. Homosexuality is the only kind of buddy ship in the Legion,"

"Have you ever thought of escaping?"

"That's all you ever think about. Not a chance. If I buy a shirt or a pair of shoes my company commander will know it right away. It would be hell to explain what you need it for as the Legion dresses you. I am off today and can do what I please but only here in Beni Ounif. I could go out through that door and continue right out of town. How far would I get? Not further than it would take for some buddy to run up to headquarters to collect the info money. From there it is a direct trip to Colomb Bechar and that is a place where you can forget both watch and almanac."

Colomb Bechar, the entry point to the desert, is also where the Legion runs a prison. It was obviously fairly simple to land there, but apparently not so simple to get out of there.

Hotel Trans Saharienne in Beni Ounif had a twin in Colomb Bechar. Once, the French had plans to build a railroad across the desert all the way down to Mali and French Sudan. They started with the stations, but they never got to lay the rails. So, from the station in Colomb Bechar there are also four stations to the south. The project was apparently stopped because French shipping companies had no interest in a desert line to take business away from their shipping routes to the colonies.

A large portion of the population in Colomb Bechar was in the Foreign Legion prison. The rest seemed to spend most of their time strolling up and down the quarter mile long Avenue Poincarre when they had nothing else to do. It seemed that they had nothing else to do most of the time. Busiest in Colomb Bechar were the prostitutes, prison guards, and convoy truckers.

Colomb Bechar was the launching pad for convoys crossing the desert and the commandant ruled the passage. We took our papers from Algiers to him. He told us that sure our papers were in order, but in his opinion neither our vehicle nor we were fit for the Sahara. We did not have any experience and the VW sure wasn't suitable for desert travel.

"It's my men who have to drive out there and pick you up if you get stranded and I can assure you that we damn it don't want to do that just because a couple of tourists want to prove something. Good afternoon, messieurs."

Of course, he was right. Still, we finally got him by hanging around his office until people must have seen us as part of the inventory. And he must have loved us like malaria. There were not many who believed that we would succeed until the route opened again in late autumn. But after a couple of weeks of pestering him, he yelled out: "Get out of my sight!!"
We did just that.

There were two routes across the Sahara, via Tanezrouf or via Tamanrasset. The latter was a rough, thorn filled tire eater. Tanezrouf, on the other hand, was a smooth sand plateau without defined roads across fifty percent of the way from the village of Adrar to Bidon V, and on to Niamey in French Sudan. The stretch over Tanezrouf—the land of thirst—was only marked by oil drums on top of each other ('bidons'). You just had to look out for a bidon and head for it.

It was two at night. The temperature had dropped to an agreeable 34 degrees. A mean sandy wind whipped the windscreen when suddenly we heard a noise as if someone had thrown a spanner in the engine. The bolt that held the big flywheel behind the engine had cracked and loosened. Now, we could have used Ian, who had left us in Colomb Bechar where he was able to catch a ride with a military truck the 100 miles to Adrar.

We weren't much at mechanics, Bengt and I. We studied the VW manual and searched our inventory of spare parts and found that we had one. Hallelujah!

The VW engine was attached to the chassis by four bolts. It had to be pulled out. In workshops, there were special hoists for that. Here, we just had my back. We loosened the four bolts. I slid in under the engine and backed out with it on my back. When we replaced the bolt, we found that the gasket behind the bolt had busted. And of that part, we had no spare.

"Who was the idiot," Bengt said, " who told us that this never had to be replaced?"

We filled the gasket housing with rubber pieces and prayed to God. Before we reached Adrar from where we could wire for spares, we had the engine out another frustrating six times. We had not only used up all the rubber pieces we could find, but also the leather straps of our watches. We sat in Adrar several weeks waiting for a military plane to arrive with a gasket, staying at the station built for the railroad that never materialized. It was a big empty building on, the outskirts of the small town laid out around a square the size of a couple of football fields. We slept on the roof and during the days, we did like the Arabs, stayed inside doing nothing. Temperatures could hit 50 C, or about 110 F.

Adrar seemed to be from the story about the country where everything was the other way. It was a sandstorm whipped place built from sun-dried clay and populated by black Arabs with a meharist captain (Méhariste, a term originating in French for the camel cavalry), a mayor, a doctor who also functioned as a veterinarian for camels and a stationmaster without trains.

We were told that once, nineteen years ago, it rained in Adrar. The children scared by water from heaven when it was supposed to be taken from wells in the ground, were frightened and hid as some of the mud buildings melted away in the rain. The old people said the rain was Allah's weeping over their sins. How could water come from the heavens when you had to dig for it in the ground?

The captain - the Chef d'Ánnexe - ruled the place. Fanned by an Arab boy, he sat in his mud fort. Without him no legal matter could be solved, no wells dug, no houses built. He was a meharist and the only people he had no power over were his own soldiers. The meharists took over south of Colomb Bechar when the French felt it was too hot for the Legion. They were camel riders who owned their animals, weapons and equipment, and they paid their own upkeep from their salaries. Many regarded them as the best soldiers in the world. They were not bound by any written contracts. They joined when they felt like it and quit when they wanted. For an méhariste, distances and heat meant nothing. As we inquired if he had any news about the plane coming from Algiers with his relief officer, he pointed at a sign on the wall behind him. It said Patience cést ma Force (Patience is my strength).

The meharists were the desert guides, the well finders, and the police. They rode in patrols of three and stayed out in the desert six months of the year. They guarded the frontiers and the water holes and pursued smugglers' caravans. Today they are the inner strength of the Algerian desert army.

An Méhariste-Pisteur, a tracker and guide, knew every water hole in a desert land as big as the state of Florida. Where you can stand a hundred feet away from a water hole and not see it, a pisteur will hit it right on from tens of miles. His "road signs" are a dip in a mountain chain far away, a couple of stones placed upon each other, bones from dead camels, the color shift in the sand, a car wreck; these are all like a road map to a pisteur.
Such a pisteur was Moubediane. When we asked him how he knew exactly where there was a water hole far away, he said: "I passed there with my father when I was seven."

The desert Arab never forgets an area that he has traveled in one time.

The only bar in Adrar was in the Hotel Djemila. The host was a Corsican, Andreadi. He rolled out the hotel beds onto the veranda every evening. Once a week, the bar buzzed with life. A gang of workers from a water-drilling project to fertilize a large area came to town with a bang. The foreman was a Russian who looked like a giant twin brother of Clark Gable. When Andreadi heard the blast of the truck horn, he opened the double doors to the bar. Ivan drove his truck loaded with a dozen water drillers right up to the bar. If he saw a stranger at the bar, as Bengt and I, he shook his beer bottle and, laughing, drenched them. When his workers were all properly drunk, he physically loaded them back on the truck bed and went back inside until every man was out, except he. Once everyone had been loaded on the truck bed he took off and returned to the desert until next week's binge.

Andreadis' "hotel" or whatever you might call it, was a stinker both in air and price, but it was the only place in Adrar where you could get a cold drink.

When we went across to the captain and wondered if he had heard anything about the flight and when we might expect it, he just shook his head, pointed at the patience sign on the wall and said: "Ici, messieurs, cést le Sahara."

Water, shade and patience are all that are of any importance in the desert.

The doctor in Adrar was part of the French administration. He had chosen to become a desert doctor. He could have opened a practice in France making a good living. Instead, he ran this desert "hospital". His workload was probably the heaviest south of the coast; half of it would probably floor a doctor in France. He had himself taught his two Arab helpers the rudiments of nursing. He would take an appendix, or pull a wisdom tooth right after bandaging a Méhariste camel. He would operate on trachoma patients a couple of times a week. Trachoma, if not operated on, causes blindness. Eighty percent of the desert population was in those days victimized by the infectious disease. His hospital had 37 beds but never less than double that amount of patients. The families of the patients camped outside and cooked all the meals, although there was a kitchen for special cases. He handled all the medical equipment, like X-ray machines, himself. If electricity failed, he was the one to work on the diesel generator. Twice a month, he toured the oases with small dispensaries in his district - a trip of about 200 miles.

When I asked him why he chose to become a desert doctor, he simply answered: "My father was a desert doctor."

He took a vacation once in France. After a week, he left what he saw as a too fast lifestyle and returned to North Africa. He spent the rest of his vacation visiting desert doctors.

While in Adrar we learned how to ride a camel. We soon found that your behind is always on its way down when the camel's hump is on its way up. In the beginning, it's a most painful meeting. The camels never showed any great interest in us. As a matter of fact, camels never show anything of anything for anyone. They go with anybody. If their master dies, they don't care a hoot. When they themselves die, they just lie down suddenly and die quickly like this is none of your business.

Abd el Krim sort of adopted us. He could have been about eight or nine, maybe a bit more, but he was not quite clear about it himself. When we ate, he sat a couple of meters away. When we slept, he would curl up in a corner. If I woke up in the middle of the night, he was right there with the water bottle. For him, the car and we constituted the big adventure. He went around among his friends telling them that he was allowed to sit in the car and even hold the steering wheel. Now and then, he allowed his friends to come to the entrance to the station and look at the car as he sat in it. One thing he found hard to understand was why I kept showing a photograph of my wife. For him, it would have been much more natural if the picture had been of my dog or horse.

It was, of course, inevitable that sooner or later, one way or another, we were going to leave Adrar. The gasket arrived coinciding with an Arabic truck convoy that did not need to bother about any permits. We decided to hang on to it. But we had to sign a paper saying that if we, in any way shape or form, delayed the convoy more than three hours; we had to abandon the Volkswagen right there and then.

Abd el Krim came to us just before we left. He gave us a gerba of goatskin in which to keep water. You drink from one of the legs. We hung it outside and the draft from driving cooled the water. It wasn't the most sanitary, but brown particles of goatskin and foul taste were, of course, bagatelles when you were thirsty in the desert.

"Allah will one day lead you back here because his grace is great. Until then, a part of my heart will be with you on the road."

They sure have a way to express themselves in the desert. A rare treat for a Swede whose children bid farewell with a reminder to bring something home from the trip...

After about 100 miles we passed the last military outpost at Reggan. From there on south, it was empty desert without roads for 600 miles - a sea of sand. The head of the convoy looked at us in such a way that I wondered if he and his driving buddies might have had a poker game about our equipment when we broke down. I think he found it inevitable. The Tanezrouft, a region of Sahara in southern Algeria and northern Mali, has taken many lives.

We decided to try to keep ahead of the convoy. The trucks were slower than us and now and then had to stop facing the wind to keep their engines from overheating. We had no water-cooling system. With thicker oil, our air-cooled engine just kept running.

To begin with, the road had been a camel created trail. Soon followed a stretch for several hundred miles, which consisted of a belt, sometimes several miles long, of mixed ground. There were big loose sand patches interspersed with areas of packed sand covered by a crust, like the crust on snow. The technique was to seek out the hard areas that were different in color and then floor the gas pedal and drive as fast as you could as the crust broke behind you. Slowing down meant that you sank through and got stuck. As you looked out for drivable areas you also had to look out for the big bidons that marked the way south. There was a fifty liter gasoline drum marking every kilometer, a 200 liter drum every five kilometer and two 200 liter ones on top of each other every ten kilometers. We kept cruising sometimes further to the side than forward.

One of the Arab drivers, who apparently felt a bit sorry for us, gave us a couple of road tips before we set out. "When you have passed balise 60, look out. There is the skeleton of a camel. Turn sharp right there because there is a difficult passage ahead. When you reach some body parts from a Berliot truck, you turn sharp south until you reach the rear part of a DC 3 plane that crashed there four years ago and twenty passengers died from thirst".

He also said that if we were lost, we should circle until we found a spot hard enough to hold us and then take out new directions.

We were now in an area where the founder of the Méhariste regiment, General Lapparinne, died from thirst. The last words in his logbook were: "I thought I knew the Sahara."

For every forward mile, it seemed that we went two miles sideways. When we reached what our convoy friend called terre pourrie, rotten ground, we had to haul out the sand mats. I don't remember if they were thirty or forty-five feet long, but I remember they were heavy and hot as hell. We used rags to handle them. Once you got the mats under the wheels, you might be able to drive a 300 feet or less before you got stuck again. Then you had to walk back and collect the mats that weighed twenty-five kilo apiece, and put them under the wheels again. The night saw us stuck several times.

We had managed to stay ahead of the convoy and could see the lights from the other trucks at the horizon behind us. We were now entering the darker, clay-based areas of fech fech where we had to keep an even speed to pass over the thin crust. The slightest variation of the gas pedal made the wheels break the crust and get us stuck in the pulverized soil underneath. You not only had to avoid the slightest speed change, you also had to avoid tracks from other vehicles, or even camels. At night, in order to see a gasoline barrel, we had to come within three hundred feet.

I remembered that the captain in Adrar had told us that the best way to get lost in the Sahara is to drive through the fech fech of Tanezrouf during nighttime.

We used a wrench to keep the gas pedal steady. We missed one of the drums six times in the dark. Finally, when morning broke, we found it. We had then been driving back and forth and around for eight hours in second gear. Without getting stuck a single time! It was a fantastic feat; a triumph for the air-cooled engine.

The fech fech ended and we could now set our sights on Bidon V, Poste Maurice Cortier. It was marked on the map with an airfield, gas pump, water tower and telegraph so you would think it was a big place, The airfield was a sand strip; the gas tank was empty; the water had dried up. The Legion telegraph operator and an Arab guard had left. BidonV was only open about half the year.

When we arrived, it was closed due to the heat. It was too hot even for the Legion.

Bidon V was the fifth big drum assembly north of Tessalit. The first to cross the Land of Thirst was a Captain Cortier with three men and eight camels in 1913.

We were about 150 miles from Tessalit and we looked over our water supply. Yes, we actually had enough to allow us to wash up - if we shared.

The sterile flatland behind us slowly disappeared. Now, that lifeless flatland changed into a step of thorn bushes.

Finally Tessalit! And water! There was even a small pool. Bengt plunged in bouncing around gregariously like a walrus in heat. Then he sat down in a corner and said he would stay there until he could collect social security.

After Tessalit, we could unload our steel mats and sell off half of the jerry cans we had used for water. It was as if the bus had taken a deep sigh of relief as it straightened up the rear wheels that had been leaning outwards.

From the old castle hill in Bourem, we saw the lights and fires down by the river. It was our first night in black Africa. Melancholic sounding drums sent their rhythms down the Niger River to the big bend. It was also the first time we listened to Africa's drums. This was part of what I had been dreaming about as a boy.

A hyena yelped and a jackal howled down by the river. Somewhere in the dark water you could hear a group of hippos roaming around. The day was dead, but the night lived on with a thousand sounds. Above us were a bluish black heaven full of glittering stars and a moon that picked out the contours of the landscape.

The drums carry the message of offers to the gods. Because of this, the drum is a holy thing in West Africa and the drummer has a special place in the blacks' world. An African may reach any position in life, move away from a primitive life, to a city, study, become both a Christian and a political big wig - but the drum continues to play a fundamental part in his life.

In many stories telling the history of a tribe, the drummer is named first, ahead of the hunter and the blacksmith. It was the drummer who called elders together and the warriors to war, warned about approaching dangers and created the lusting at festivities and the sadness at funerals. Without the drummer, no medicine man could work and no chief feel important. When a drummer dies, the belief is that his soul comes to rest in his old drums. If there is no one designated to inherit the drums, they become taboo. Most black African religions are built on the belief of the power that exists in the air, the earth, the trees, the plants, the stones and the big waters.

It was 60 miles in muddy wheel tracks to Gao. It was like driving a tram. The French had a habit of placing customs in the midst of their colonies. That way, they saved staffing costs. After Gao the road was so bad that it was easier to drive on the side of it, and I bet that hasn't changed since. It was so muddy and slippery that we turned and skidded and felt as if we were attached to the tip of the wagging tail of a big dog.

It is not, I can assure you, my intention to speak badly about Attawel Ibrahim, the Arab Hausa chief, whose hospitality was great and whose title was Chef du Canton de Dogderraoua of the land towards the border to Nigeria.

If Attawel had lived some generations earlier, he would most likely have been one of the great slave trade suppliers. He owned a white horse and a saddle clothed in leopard skin as well as several camels. He had the four wives allowed in the Koran and changed them now and then. The ones he discarded were sent off to be marketed. He liked his wives to be between 12 and 17.

Ibrahim's adjutants had stopped us on the road and invited us to the residency which was the only two story building in the village. In the big ground floor room Attawel sat on the floor, two wives on each side, in front of a wall covered from floor to ceiling with filled ground nut sacks - the product that made him a rich man. The room was full of adjutants as he called them. We walked inside, shoes in hand, dirty khaki shirts, months of unshaven faces and he addressed us as follows:

"How are you? How are your sons? Are your brothers in good health? How is your horse? How is your camel?" He did not ask about our women because no one could have any interest in how they were doing.

The audience did not take long. Attawel left us in the hands of his son Kadri Attawel who held the position as Secretaire du Chef de Canton de Doguerraoua. We made him understand that we felt it was a very impressive position.

Villagers crowded around our bus as Kadri took us to the back of the house and showed us a room on the second floor for our stay. Obviously, without asking us, they had decided that we should stay. Kadri fixed straw carpets for bedding and a servant came with beautifully ornate calabashes filled with rice and legs of lamb fried in pillipilli that would have made a curry trained Indian jump in the lake. Not even the flies wanted it. When we sort of hinted at the unusual sharpness, Kadri said:

"Very Good. Kills all worms."

We sat outside the room and wondered what on earth we were doing there. The sun went down and Kadri came to ask if it now was dark enough to roll up the screen and start showing our films.

"We have no films."

"All missionaries show films."

"We are not missionaries."

"But you have the beards of missionaries!"

Bengt and I had grown some long unruly beards in the desert. The kind they call missionary beards in Africa. How could we save the situation?

I found myself explaining it as a curiosity of where we came from.

"Kadri, we have beards because where we come from it is so cold all the time that we have to have beards. Even the children and women have beards. We are here to make films to show them at home a land where children and women don't have to have beards."

Incredibly, he believed me but stressed that no filming of women was allowed. Maybe he accepted explanations simply out of courtesy or to cover up his mistake. "Of course, he said, "Now I understand fully." That's when we rolled out the KAK scroll filled with impressive stamps, signatures and ribbons. He took it to his father to sign on the same page as the chieftain of this strange land where the cold forces women and children to wear facial hair. His father was so impressed by the scroll that he decided that Bengt and I should have two girls for the night: two 13-year-old beauties. They had just been given a bath and they came innocently smiling with their teeth red from betel chewing.

Now how would we get out of this one?

"Your women are beautiful, Kadri, and it is a great honor you are showing us."

"Are you not Attawel Ibrahim's guests?"

"It is with great sadness, Kadri, that we have to deny ourselves the pleasure of this extraordinary gesture of hospitality. But as you have a Ramadan with rules that cannot be broken, we have something similar. It does not restrict our eating but demands a total abstinence from women for two months. We are in that period now." Kadri once again seemed to swallow my nonsense. He most likely thought that from a country with bearded women, you could expect anything.

We had found that the best gift we could give our African friends were laxatives. Astra, the medical company in Södertälje (now British merged and called Astra Zeneca) had provided us with enough laxatives for a regiment. When we presented Ibrahim with one hundred of the finest laxatives, he felt he owed us a party. To my surprise, he allowed Bengt to take a photo of him with his three brides. It was to be taken in his bedroom because that was the only place where Allah allowed him sexual freedom. By the way, his huge bed was the only piece of furniture in the house.

Kadri recommended a trip to meet the chieftain in Tahoua, about 90 miles out on the steppe. It was a large village. It looked like a cut off anthill shared between Tuaregs and the permanent black Arabica. The chief was an old man - of course with young wives. He drank a lot of beer, a quarter of a gallon bottle at a time.

His throne room, or whatever you may want to call it, had walls decorated with the most beautiful calabashes. I asked if I could buy one. He did not reply so I figured that perhaps he was expecting a bid.

"I'll gladly pay a hundred francs for that one", I offered. No reply made me think my bid was too low.

"Two hundred francs," I said.

"I like your shirt," he said. "Would you sell it?"

"I may. What do you bid?" Thinking this was more likely sort of a swap, I repeated, "How much do you bid?"

"A hundred thousand francs."

"For my shirt! Are you, are you kidding?"

"Two hundred thousand, perhaps? Who am I to put a price on your belongings?"

We left feeling that an old man in a desert land had taught us some manners. I remember it clearly to this day.

We had heard that there should be a rich wild life around Tahoua: antelopes, giraffes, lions, and elephants.

On the road again, we stopped frequently to look for animals. Not much luck.

It was, of course, disappointing. But the fact is that already fifty years ago and more you had to go to East Africa for zoology. The West African coast belt was too heavily populated and the inland not friendly to big game any more. Our route so far had been in the company of scorpions, hyenas and some desert dogs.

In Africa, a bad road could be worse than anything you have ever seen. There are fewer good roads in Africa today than during the colonial years. Too many conflicts have left much of the infrastructure in shambles. The leaders think more about padding their bank accounts in Switzerland than repairing a bridge over the Ituri River in the Congo.

From the Nigerian border we were heading south to the emirate capital of Kano. From there we had a long drive to the coast and the capital city of Lagos. There we had taken upon ourselves to conduct a seminar about Volkswagen at the first VW dealership in Africa: Mandelas and Karaberis. Our VW was the first to be seen in Africa. The dealership had not yet received the first shipload.

But first we wanted to have a look at the emirate capital of Kano. We took a room at a small hotel to shower, shave, get our laundry done, and to stretch out between some clean sheets for the first time in months. At about three in the morning, I woke up feeling that there was someone in the room; a shadowy figure in a corner. Bengt jumped him, but he slipped Bengt's rugby tackle and my grip and ran. The old African trick of smearing the body with oil had worked once again.

All our money was gone. Over and done with it seemed. But the briefcase that had held it was still there, which proved to us that the thieves must be among the reception staff who saw the content of the briefcase when we checked in.

The Ascaris, the British black police constables, came and made notes. Then a British police officer came, made more notes and had three double whiskies at the bar, cursed the climate and promised to see what he could do; which of course turned out to be nothing.

We now had between us exactly three shillings, eight pence and a couple of stamps from French Sudan. Not a very pretty situation. Then, suddenly we had a visit by the hotel barber, a fat little man who sweated enormously. He said that he had heard about our misfortune and if we had "something" to sell, he knew a man that was interested.

By "something," we soon understood that he meant weapons. I had nothing against selling our revolvers and Husqvarna rifles because they had caused us so much bother at every border crossing that we would be better off without them. OK, maybe we should keep one.

The barber's contact was Ndumanya and he lived in a pink colored stone house in the Sabon Gari part of town where all had bicycles and someone even had an automobile. Across the street from his house was the bar, The Road to Heaven, next door to Hallelujah Groceries. We entered a room of well-polished mahogany furniture and spangle draperies. The barber sat in a chair drinking Heineken beer at ten dollars a bottle.

"Ndumanya very rich man. Builds many houses in Sabon Gari."

We nodded and the man himself looked as if it was just an incident that he had not built every house in Sabon Gari.

"Ndumanya is also a very good man. Yes sir, very good man. He give much money to the poor. Who thanks Mdumanya? Yes Sir! All want to steal money from Ndumanya, yes sir! Thief men in Kano, yes sir. God says Mndumanya must defend himself."

"So you want to buy our revolvers?"

"Yes sir, and two rifles."

They were indeed well informed. Ndumanya, who had not said anything so far, smacked his lips with joy and his eyes rolled like ping pong balls in his head. With a bit of effort, I felt we could have sold him half the Swedish army.

"Remember," he said, "this is between the four of us and the Almighty."

I don't know what God had to do with contraband. We took a sizeable advance like real crooks and next morning when we hurried out of town, we left the weapons with the British police administrator, who then, I presumed, would sort out this business with Ndumanya.

I will never forget the provincial capital Kaduna, which means crocodile in Hausa. We arrived on a Saturday. A couple of imposing (for Africa) government buildings was sleeping between perfectly raked walkways and neat brick style villas for the civil servants. Much as a kind of reminder of Kent and Surrey. This was one of Britain's largest posts in West Africa. On the porches sat families with neatly dressed children having lemonades served by bare footed black boys in white mess jackets. Someone called Kaduna the last hope of the British spinster. There were at least a dozen men to one woman, and only married men were granted a villa. So when the plane arrived from England, you would find a bunch of bachelors at the airport eyeing the female arrivals.

A friend once asked me how the British were, out there. "Exactly like in Clerkenwell-on-the-Thames, only sweatier," I said. It was old boy and three slaps on the back, jolly good show and another three slaps until the beer ran out and all walked home in the African night.

We were a wee bit of celebrities in Kaduna because they had heard over the radio about these two SWISS gentlemen who had crossed the desert from Europe by car, thereby setting a record. The message was then repeated in Hausa, Fulami and Kanuri.

The Nigerians have, ever since their independence, been busy killing each other. The Yoruba don't like the Ibo and none of them likes the Hausa. It's a bit better today but never really peaceful or even "truceful". Maybe you remember the Ibo-Yoruba war. The Swedish former air force pilot and later head of the Ethiopian imperial Air force, Count von Rosen, joined the Ibo. He got a training plane from an aircraft manufacturer in Malmö. He attached bombs under the wings, flew too low, just above the treetops, not to be hit by ground fire. He pulled a string releasing the bombs and for several months he alone held the vastly superior Yoruba troops at bay.

There are over 250 different tribes in Nigeria and none of them like each other. It has taken a couple of generations now to make them accept that they are Nigerians and not just Yoruba, Ibo, Hausa Filami, Edo, Urbobo, Efik and so on.

The religious differences have also played a big part in splitting the population. Not least since the fundamentalists who spread fear in Hausa Land have influenced the Islamic north.

There was not much the Nigerians could agree upon when decolonized. The Parliament's first majority decision was to prohibit the natives of the Jos plateau from coming into any town naked.

We had a long drive to Lagos over roads that went from non-existent to tarmac, depending on the influence of the area big wig with the British. If he was of importance and wanted a road asphalted to his second home, he got it. The result was that all over the country, there were these tarmacs from nowhere to nowhere, just so the emirs, chieftains or whoever they were of Colonial importance, could run their Jaguars comfortably.

We had to make this stop in Lagos profitable, so here we were showing professional mechanics how to service a VW. One piece of luck in all the misfortune was that we had so much mechanical trouble in the desert that we got to know every nut and bolt of the engine. Most of the grease monkeys were Africans, while the foremen were mostly Lebanese. Contrary to the custom in the French colonies where French workers did everything, no Englishman would dirty his hands with manual work in the colonies.

Greeks and Lebanese were the industrious newcomers of West Africa. The Lebanese were said to arrive with a dozen rolls of cloth, rent a hole in the wall and sleep in the back. After a year, they ran a shop. After five years, they had a house and a retirement plan to return to Lebanon.

The local European paper told the story of the two Swedes and showed some of Bengt's photos from the trip. It so impressed the owner of the hotel where we stayed, Mr. Economidas, that he wanted Bengt to take photos of him and his wife for the family in Lebanon. He ordered twenty copies and closed a bathroom on the second floor at the hotel for the exclusive use of Bengt. He spread the word about this international photographer staying at his place. Being Lebanese he did not do anything for nothing. He never really told us what he charged but claimed he kept 25% of Bengt's charges, whatever they were, which included the actual camera work. We traveled the town taking pictures and Bengt spent nights in the bathroom that had been converted into a darkroom, making copies for the friends and relatives at home in Lebanon. Guests in need after 8 PM were out of luck for the duration of our stay.

We made enough money to take us to Stanleyville in the Congo, which had Belgian banks with which we had made prior arrangements. A Sabena pilot would deliver cash directly to the bank at the airport. All we had to do was to get there.

A bit down the road in Cameroon and taking the red clay road into the Central African Republic, we spotted a Swedish flag high up on the crest of a green hill.
"Do you see what I see?" asked Bengt.
I took the binoculars and said, "You are damn right!"

When we drove up in front of the porch of the Örebro Mission's station, Svea Blom, who had seen us coming, stood waiting. Her first words were:
"I see there are some stockholmers out touring so I'd better put on the coffee."

She was totally cool after the day's work and so was her partner in Christ, Esther Skoglar, who was working in the kitchen. She had lived here over twenty years but she didn't look as if she had ever lived anywhere except in a little red house by a lake in Värmland.

We had landed in a Swedish world of meatballs, home baked bread and rag carpets. No one could see that Esther, just before we arrived, had raked down one of the world's most deadly poisonous snakes, a black mamba, from the straw roof and killed it. And no one could see that Svea, who always wore two hats, had just returned from a moped ride to a couple of outlaying villages in the bush.

In primitive areas like the one around Bouar (in the western central African Republic), adventure was part of a day's work. It was just a routine to inspect the bed to make sure that a snake or some scorpions did not take advantage of the comfort.

I once read a book by a French officer about his adventurous years at the Bouar military post. He had experienced some really dangerous things. Now, on the porch of the Swedish church, I remembered it. I talked to Svea about it because she had shared the same terrain with that officer for at least a dozen years.

"Yes," she said, "there are of course a lot of animals out there in the forest, but you always know that they are more afraid of you than you of them. I always walk with a stick. I click it on the ground and wave it in the grass making noise and the animals flee."

I understand it became pretty hard on all missionaries in Central Africa when the colonies became independent. From Tchad in the north, all the way to the South African border, new governments, unable to rule and control, found their countries terrorized by rebel troops on robbery and murder sprees. A band of only a hundred could terrorize thousands. Svea and Esther stayed at the station, but they had to close the school. The only reason they survived the years before the country had a functioning - even if brutal - government, was because some of the local area rebels had been taught to read and write by Svea and Esther.

The "white era" was peaceful in most parts of Africa south of the Sahara. No one starved, children went to school, roads were kept drivable, and bridges were repaired. But, of course, there is the old saying: "Better to govern yourself badly, than be governed well by someone else."

With many mission stations closing, practically all schools and dispensaries in the bush disappeared. The irony is that so many of the murdering despots roaming the new countries had a Christian upbringing. In countries like the Central African Republic, Gabon, and Congo Brazzaville, all educational facilities disappeared with the mission schools.

The white era was peaceful and the natives lived fairly well, but very little was actually done to further the relationships between Africans and Europeans. It was not until the 1950's that the Belgians introduced a law in the Congo that prohibited the use of the word maraca (monkey) when summoning a servant. The missionaries were not very popular among the European colonials because they were thought to be putting all sorts of ideas into the heads of the blacks, which made them more difficult to handle. In turn, the missionaries also had an ongoing fight against medicine men and witch doctors.

The French equatorial colonies were far behind France's colonies elsewhere. They were where you disposed of civil servants that caused trouble at home or in the other colonies. It was a public service dump. It had the worst roads in Africa and an unhealthy climate. The Central African Republic and Tchad were the forgotten colonies.

The Ubangi River took it slow and easy at Bangassou, the border station from where to ferry to Kongo. The rain forest grew aggressively dense. A couple of hippos lazed a bit down river and some crocodiles sort of floated by. As we boarded the "ferry" - two long planks spanning six canoes dug out from the area's big mahogany trees - kids came from all over to look at a car the likes of which they had never seen before. A couple of them had caught nightingales and tied a string around the bird's leg. The boys laughed and jumped of joy when the birds tried to fly away. When the birds gave up, they were thrown in the river.

It was quite a nervous moment to get the VW onto the ferry. The planks first had to be placed to match the wheels. We then had to drive onto them when the ferry heaved to match the shoreline. It took half an hour to have everything connected. The ferry then had to be poled up river about half a mile. Then, fifty paddlers working fiercely to the beat of drums took it across to the ferry station on the Kongo side. Now over fifty years later, I understand that they still work this crossing in the same way.

Belgian Kongo's blue flag with the yellow star flew over a small tidy brick building, well-kept lawn and beds with flowers in military parade order. What a difference to the French laissez-faire.

Kongo was eighty times the size of Belgium. I think it led the border commandant to believe that his power was also eighty times the responsibility of his colleagues in Belgium. His paper work demands were extraordinary - a form of "form-a-titis." After six hours, he knew more about Bengt, and me than we had remembered ourselves in a long time.

The Belgians were extremely ambitious in Kongo. They worked under the pressure of being a small nation with an enormously big responsibility. For this reason the country gave a better impression of law and order than any other colony south of the Sahara. The big cities had modern hotels, ladies' hair salons, dress shops and restaurants. The Belgians lived well, ate well and slept safely. They did not allow the Africans to get an education past fifth class. Most missions were catholic but there were also several Swedish missionaries working in the eastern now war ravaged places like Butembo and Usumbura. Patrice Lumumba, the first president of the independent Kongo went to the Swedish Mission School in Bukavu by the Lake Kivu.

Everything was extremely expensive in Kongo, something they blamed on lack of foreign currencies. The only thing real cheap was cigarettes. When I cabled the publisher for funds he replied: Eat less, smoke more, and drink water.

When Stanley was out looking for Emin Pasha, the leading slave trader, it took him over one year to cross the dense rain forest one step and one machete cut at a time. Today, if the road is still there, you cross it by car in a couple of days. That is, if the weather allows and the elephants don't block the road.

From Stanleyville - today Kishangani - we were ready to tackle the rain forest road. It was like driving through a tunnel of green. You could not see the sky and would not know if it rained out there or if the sun was shining. The humidity made everything moist and a fog seemed to grow out of the ground.

Almost half through the Ituri we lost the left rear wheel after we had paid a garage in Stanleyville big money to apply new brake linings. The mechanic had missed a bolt splint. So there we sat with half of our behind in the muddy mess.

I left Bengt and started walking. The map said there was a river shortly ahead and at a river there is generally a village. Then suddenly there was a sign saying "Beware of elephants". What elephants? I did not see any. But just at that moment an elephant came out from the forest. Then another. And another. Soon there were about a dozen and I was scared. My blood ran cold, I wanted to run, climb up a tree, dig a grave, cry, say boo, and stick out my tongue. Then I saw a man on top of one of the elephants. He waved at me and pointed down the road. Slowly I walked towards the river until I had the elephants behind me - and then I ran, oh did I ever run? I think the elephant rider was as stunned as I was. I mean it was not every day a white man is seen walking through the Ituri. By the river there was a camp and a sign: Station de Groupe de Capture des Okapis.

The river was Epulu, the main artery through the rain forest. The camp had been established to regulate the rain forest fauna - especially to protect the rare okapi, the world's latest discovered hoof animal. A Swedish lieutenant in the service of the Belgian colonial army by the Karl Eriksson first saw it in 1900. But the Latin name for the animal is Okapia Jonstoni after Sir Harry Johnston, the early twentieth century governor of Uganda, sadly not Okapia Erikssoni. Up until WWII the animal had been brutally pursued for sale to zoological gardens at prizes of more than $20,000. To regulate the hunt of this most rare of all hoof animals and still meet the request from zoological gardens, the Belgian government established this station at the Epulu River in the heart of okapi land. They selected an Officier du Chasse and major in the colonial army, Jean de Medina, an African-Portuguese to head the station. He developed a technique to capture the okapis without losing any. He let them catch themselves. He created paths in the forest lined with the plants the okapis fed on. They walked the path right up onto his truck. He drove them to the station and kept them there for a year to get used to people before shipping them to zoos all over the world.

Medina had a hobby - to train elephants. When he was told that the African elephant could not be tamed he simply said: "Hannibal did it".

It was Medina's elephants I met on the road. Medina sent a couple of men with Bengt and an elephant to pull our VW to the station.

I have met many remarkable people in my life, but few have made a deeper impression on me than this Portuguese mulatto. He was a big man, about six feet and 250 lbs. But he moved through the dense forest like a cat. He had built his bungalow around a huge mahogany tree on which he hung his many rifles. A pet lion, Simba, rested at his feet and followed him like a dog.

He used his elephants to clear the forest, clean up the road and haul timber when they built the first bridge over the crocodile infested Epulu River. In 2009 on the Discovery channel on TV I saw an episode of a woman being mauled by a crocodile in the Epulu River. Across the road from Medina's station was a small room and breakfast place. It was all built with bamboo cut right out of the forest. There were ten rooms, a bar and a dining veranda. Wherever you were you could see the sky between the bamboos. It was the only rooming place before you hit the border to Uganda.

One day when we sat on the porch, Medina heard an elephant trumpeting. He said, oh my god that's Ngara. I wondered how he could know what elephant it was. He looked at me with the look of "you don't know much do you?"

Ngara had been a young work elephant. One day she took off with a work chain around her body. Now her body had grown, but the chain had not. Medina duly reported to the superiors in Stanleyville, who ordered him to truck in the elephant for veterinarian care.

The vets in Stanleyville could not do much. The damage was too severe. Medina was told that the elephant would be destroyed. Medina protested and went to Stanleyville to pick up Ngara declaring that if the elephant had to be killed he would be the only one to do it.

Medina took Ngara back to Epulu. He let her lose in the forest. She walked into the forest to a small opening with a muddy patch. There she spruced the mud over her wound. Medina had followed her and for almost two weeks he stayed by Ngara and kept talking to her. He sat there outside his tent and looked at her across the mud pond. She stood on the other side and looked at him while now and then munching on leaves from the eucalyptus trees. He paid pygmies to bring wild bananas. The two understood each other. When Medina felt that the wound had healed enough he went over to Ngara, grabbed her behind an ear and said, "let's go home." And off they went. She just followed him.

The pygmies, the small people, the Bambutis, or whatever they are called in various parts of central Africa, live deep in the rainforest. They come out to the road for the few supplies they need from the people of the villages who are called "Arabisé". They came a long time ago from Muslim countries like Zanzibar to hunt for slaves, hence the name. They soon found that by enslaving the pygmies they had the forest hunters supplying their villages with meat.

Medina liked the small people, about 135 centimeters (4'4") tall. On Saturday nights when Medina ran some old 16 mm movies on a sheet he rigged on the porch for himself and his crew, the pygmies turned up to sit in front of the sheet. Medina liked westerns. He borrowed them from the Catholic mission station in Mambasa. The pygmies probably did not understand much of what they saw, but every time a white man shot another white man they clapped and laughed. It was mainly old westerns that I had seen on Sunday matinees at the Karla cinema in Stockholm for 35 öre (5¢).

One day, a film expedition arrived from Hollywood to collect atmosphere for a Tarzan movie. Medina was not familiar with Tarzan, so when the short and balding director said, "Hello mister Medina, I thought you would enjoy to meet Tarzan." Medina asked "Who?"

When I explained that Tarzan was a white man who lived in the jungle, swinging between the trees and hauling like a baboon, he recommended the fellow to find good psychiatric care – the sooner the better. The expedition left, never to be seen again.

Some miles from Medina's camp, a failed medical student from Boston, Patrick Putnam, had built a camp to study the life of the pygmies, Putnam Camp. He was there already before the war carrying a dream of studying and cataloging the life of the forest people. He freed many of them from their enslavement by the Arabise'.

The pygmies soon came to regard him as a god. He received medicine from the United States and opened a small dispensary for the pygmies. After the war he took a trip to America and found an artist lady who came back with him as his wife. She became deeply involved with the forest people, staying away with them for weeks at a time. She was the one who put Putnam Camp on the map, so to say. Thanks to her contacts with the outside world the camp received many famous visitors. Putnam had a drug problem from years in the Far East. He died when we were there on our second trip to Africa. Mrs. Putnam was nowhere to be found. We discovered Putnam lying in his hut, parts of his disassembled truck hanging around. The floor was full of bottles and a couple of snakes. He died shortly thereafter. We took his body to the Mission station in Mambasa. In her later book Madami about her eight years with the pygmies Mrs. Putnam noted Instead of the famous film stars, Kate and Bogey, the next visitors were two Swedish men, doing Africa on a minimum budget and hoping to make money selling stories about their travels when they got back to Stockholm.

She makes no mention in her book about his death. We were there and for reasons unknown to me she was not. His body was brought to the Catholic Mission in Mambasa about five miles away. The church filled with natives. The Song of the Parrot from a thousand voices carried Putnam to heaven.

A couple of years later when I returned to Medina's camp I found the Putnam Camp sign by the car path. I found his main building, open on all sides. On the fireplace in the middle, a big mahogany clog was burning, guarded by three Bambutis. Putnam's sleeping hut was untouched but everything else was gone.
As an answer to my question about the fire, they said that they always kept the log burning as preparation for Putnam's return.

"But Putnam is dead," I said.

"No," they said, "Putnam can not die. He is just visiting God and will be back".

From where comes this human splinter? The ancient King Herod talks about pygmies that lived in the Libyan Desert. Aristotle wrote that they lived far away in the swamps where the River Nile disappears. They are pictured in old Egyptian monuments. They might have been Africa's, or at least Central Africa's first inhabitants. Eventually the Negroes drove the pygmies to seek safety in the rain forests where no one else could live.

The forest pygmy is half nomadic, moving with his prey. He is about a meter twenty five to thirty-five with an out of proportion big head, long arms and short legs. He builds his low round hut by putting some sticks in the ground and covers them with banana leaves.

Some pygmies during the last century mixed with the Arabisé in the Ituri forest. It resulted in "pygmoids" who live close to the villages. They are about a foot taller than Bambuties. Some of them even live in the villages.

The Ituri road was kept drivable. It was the only link between Stanleyville (Kisangani) and the food producing eastern Kongo. The native drivers removed the pedal platform from the accelerator and kept only the pin, which they gripped between their toes. When you heard a truck coming you'd better get off the road. They had just one speed: full throttle, fast ahead.

If a Congolese truck broke down it was rarely rescued. It was just left in the woods for anyone to plunder. The driver took as many parts he could from the engine, put them in a sack and walked away hoping to make a few francs off of them in the next village.

Every ten miles or so the road through the forest came to a brook, You had to cross on two thick planks, which you had to adjust to the distance between your wheels. The big trucks did not care much about that. They just plowed through.

The government did a fair maintenance, as the road was the supply link from the gardens in the east to the consumers in the Stanleyville area. There were two well-engineered bridges, one about fifty meters long across the Epulu River. One day when sitting on Medina's porch we heard the approach of a big truck pulling some heavy load. It entered the bridge. The driver's part had the front wheel on the other side when the bridge collapsed with the trailer part hanging freely. The driver climbed out and looked confused. Medina cried out to him:

"What weight did you carry?"

"Twenty-five tons, bwana."

"But didn't you see the sign saying that the bridge was limited to 20 tons?"

"Yes bwana, I saw that".

"But then you knew that the bridge could only take maximum twenty tons."

"Yes bwana, I knew, but I did not know that the bridge knew..."

And don't forget that if an African happened to land on the side of the road with his truck it was not his fault. It was because the truck had jo-jo. The best you could do when you heard one of these trucks coming was to get off the road and stay there until it passed. The earlier described "pin between the toes" driving technique was combined with putting the truck in third gear in the morning and leave it there until parking for the night.

We had stayed long with Jean de Medina. You don't drop a wheel in Africa without consequences but it was time to move on. Now the road led south to the part of Africa that Livingstone explored and where Stanley found him on the shores of Lake Tanganyika. We were heading for the land of Katanga where the Belgian royal family was sole owner of the greatest treasure chest in the world - copper, diamonds and gold galore.

We stopped at Kisenyi and Goma on the northern tip of the Lake Kivu. There is no rival to the beauty of the volcano-framed lake in which the crystal clear waters let the volcanoes play a color symphony every night. This very same lake around which later millions have been murdered and where the war lords rule and governments are powerless. It was a Shangri La later turned into a hell. Yes, it was indeed a Shangri La with a climate year around like the French Riviera in the spring. The hot sandy winds from the savannas in the east and the steaming rains from the forest in the north and west never had the strength to make it over the 5000 feet high volcanic chain.

It was not the first time that this paradisal area erupted in violence during the last forty to fifty years. The area had since pre-colonial time been one of the cruelest in Africa. West of the Lake Kivu lived maniema, cannibals of pleasure who loved to kill people and eat them while dancing and singing. East of the lake were the Watutsi, hamites with a pedigree from the early Egypt, gorgers of torture and blood orgies. It did not take long for the hatred to brew over once the Belgians left Kongo and the U.N. recreated the old Rwanda Burundi. The result was one of the worst genocides in human history, a genocide that since then has spread under warlords into eastern Kongo.

During the colonial era the hills of eastern Kongo had become a great horticultural area supplying the country with fruit, vegetables and dairy products. It was also a garden of flowers for African homes. A commercial center developed at the south end of Lake Kivu, Bukavu that became one of the most elegant cities in Central Africa. But it was expensive, with sky-high prices, as almost everything had to be flown in. The only things that did not cost much were flowers and cigarettes.

In 1945 about 300 Europeans lived in Bukavu. Two years later the town had 1,571 and in the last big year before decolonizing there were 3,588. In the free Kongo, Bukavu's white population went down by half. Five years later, the African population, after doubling a couple of times, reached 40,000. The native part of town called Belch, and not without reason, was transformed in a few years, from being a nice native area with good homes, into a town of beer, sweat and tears. And garbage! For many of the Africans living in misery, the Swedish Mission station became a savior. Lewi Petrus Pentecostal Church in Stockholm saved many lives through its dispensary in Bukavu and sub stations in Usumbora in Rwanda and in Valikale. The mission school in Bukavu was where Patrice Lumumba, the Father of the Kongo state and its first president graduated.

Central Africa was, and remains, a bizarre world. It will take generations to bring peace and prosperity to countries like Kongo, and the Central African Republic. The Belgians had some trouble in Kongo before the independence. Thousands of Africans were killed in the east region when Bengt and I sat on Medina's porch.
No one heard or knew about it at the time.

We met Emma, the daughter of a local banker, when we stayed at the Swedish mission in Bukavu while working on the VW. We invited her in for dinner and then took her to the movies. I later took her to a dance. The next weekend Bengt and I together with the local Swedish missionary couple Söderberg were invited to a garden party at Emma's parents' place. Everyone in town was there and seemed eager to talk with Bengt and me about the trip. And not just the trip but what we did when we did not do what we did just then. Emma walked around giggling. Bengt and I were downing fine European beer, a rare luxury for us at ten dollars a bottle. Then Emma's father called everyone's attention - announcing Emma's engagement, to me!

Bengt was about to set a $10 Heineken in his throat. I was about to die. Emma just came rushing and giggling threw her in my arms. She had totally misunderstood the situation or was she just desperate to find a man to take her back to Europe? Staying at the Swedish mission, I felt they should have warned me that in Africa a girl couldn't date without a future aspiration. You just don't take a girl out to a dance in Africa.

I said, damn you Söderberg. The pastor must sure have been aware of the consequences. But who knows, maybe he also got a kick out of it?

"Damn you Söderberg!" I said again. He laughed and said that it "might be best for you boys to blow town in the morning. Real early I might suggest."

Bengt and I had played along during the party. There was not much else we could do. But the next morning, as Söderberg advised us, we blew town very early.

It was half an hour to sunup when we drove out of Bukavu and prized our luck that we had enough gas and provisions before having to stop for a while. I hoped that Emma would understand. Do you think she did?

To drive fast on bad African roads required special driving skills that could only be acquired through practice. One of the most important things is to learn how to anticipate what's ahead, to read the road. To know what you can expect the next half a mile or so and adjust your speed accordingly. Telltale signs came from the terrain, the trees, the groundcover, the kinds of bushes etc. If you are on a road through grassy fields and you begin to see bushes you can expect a softer road, which in turn means deeper wheel tracks. When the road makes a wide bend without any seeming reason it is looking for a place to cross a river. Clusters of trees indicate the presence of a small stream without bridge. The bigger the trees and wider apart indicates a bridge ahead. When the road surface turns to harder gravel and starts to climb, you can expect a native village within a mile or so. Then you better slow down instead of speeding on the better surface because a village means goats and dogs on the road. Hitting a goat can cost a lot before they let you pass. The natives always build their villages - regardless if it's in Nigeria or Tanganyika, on a surface that dries the fastest after a rainy period.

We still had over a thousand miles left in Kongo and its richest province, Katanga. Coming through a forested area at the southern end of Lake Tanganyika As we passed a couple of control posts, we became an object for the gold control police. They were so efficient that I'm surprised that they did not dust the tires for gold. The road passed through an area where natives stood by the roadside and sold matchboxes filled with gold dust. The road was open in one direction only on odd versus even days.

Our last event in Kongo was when we had to stop at a rain barricade outside Jadotville. Suddenly beside us stood this woman. She balanced a bucket on her head. It was big enough to wash a two year old in. It was full of rice and upon that she had a sack. A small child slept on her back with his head hanging like a thirsty tulip. Around her buzzed thousands of flies attracted by her open infected leg wounds.

Bwana nipa mgonjwakitoa duda ya mgua yangu.

She asked for help, but what could we do? Most of all we wanted to get away but we were stuck. If she does not move, Bengt said, I'll throw up. I told him to try spraying her with our DDT. It could not make her worse than she already was.

We almost regretted doing it because when the people around her saw the flies dropping they almost stormed the bus to get sprayed. Then, when we ran out of DDT they became aggressive and started to shake the VW. We had to choose between being pushed into the ditch or to force the boom. We crashed through the boom. After half a mile we had a Belgian officer on our tail.

"I have to fine you the cost of the boom, 500 francs," he said.

While he made notes, looked at our papers, inspected

the van, Bengt kept taking pictures of him at work. As I counted out the five hundred, Bengt gave him the roll of film to send home to relatives in Belgium. He took the money, gave me a receipt and then turned around and gave the money to Bengt for the film.

Entering Northern Rhodesia, today's Zimbabwe, was like leaving the real Africa. Mining projects and large farms called for good roads. There was also a different type of Europeans. The mining machinery, like bucket dredgers etc., was handled by miners from Wales who lived in simple houses. They drank beer and threw darts at the pub and did not make enough money to afford a car or even the lesser cost of a houseboy. Their Africa was the copper mining fields and a Tsetse ravaged dried up steppe bush.

Beyond the mines was the cultivated land with big farms producing enough wheat to feed the rest of Africa. It was a well run country facing less racial problems than South Africa until Robert Mugabe came to power and claimed the land back from the European settlers who had farmed there for generations. Mugabe succeeded in turning a healthy and wealthy nation in less than twenty years into a poorhouse where people die of starvation on the side of the road. Idi Amin in Uganda might have been a sadistic brute but at least he only tortured and killed those he didn't like. Mugabe indiscriminately allowed military brutes and starvation to create mass deaths. Mugabe and his generals ordered new uniforms for $2,000 a piece from tailors on Bond Street in London on which they could hang all the showy decorations they issued to each other. All while the people starved to death.

We headed for Bulavayo, passed villages of square huts and women who sat in the shade with their Swedish Husqvarna sewing machines.

We stayed a couple of days in Johannesburg, which

was as lively as New York at 10 pm but at eleven as dead as the town of Vetlanda in rural Sweden after the last movie. The road from Johannesburg to Cape Town was as inspiring as a movie I had seen five times before.

The most exciting part of any long journey is just before you arrive at your destination. On February 25, around noon, an honorary escort from the Royal Automobile Club of South Africa met us a few miles before Cape Town. They met a dirty, dented VW on tires worn to the thread.

When we arrived at the final destination, The Table Mountain, Africa's most southern point, we had set a world long distance record. It had never been a question of a race to get there but of endurance. So we looked at the baboons that rule the mountain and headed back to town and an appreciation dinner in our honor by the RAC.

On the way back into town we stopped at a city mailbox when I felt a hand on my shoulder.

"Hello Mr. Ottoson, what are you doing in Cape Town?" It was my secretary from the years at Ford in Stockholm. She had married a South African

We had driven 58,800 kilometers through 34 countries, used 77,000 liters of gasoline 385 liters of oil and worn out six tires with four half worn. And how much had this trip cost? Let's just forget that part, shall we.

HEADING HOME

Now we had to get home. We had not paid much attention to that. Should we catch a Swedish ship in Durban, South Africa, or drive all the way back now when we were familiar both with the route and the hazards? Or maybe sort of jump the east coast by boat. There was so much more to see on this fascinating continent.

We decided on "ship hopping" up along the east coast. We first boarded a ship in Durban. Our first stop became Mogadishu in Mozambique, which the Portuguese colonized four hundred years ago. It was tough going on roads they had not maintained for at least one hundred years. They were so corrugated that, if you looked up, the landscape appeared like a film stuck in the projector with the picture jumping on the screen.

We wanted to get a glimpse of the port of Sofala that was the chief seaport for gold and ivory to the Orient in Biblical times. Some mean that Sofala is the Ofir of the Old Testament, where King Solomon filled his ships with gold, silver, ivory, monkeys and peacocks.

Already during the 1920's and 30's wild life preservationists warned against elephant extinction as over 60,000 animals were killed every year for the ivory. When the authorities finally, in the 1960's, took control of the situation, the herds recovered up the African east cost but are now endangered again. The rhino population became almost extinct. The pills made from the rhino's horn are perceived as a strong sexual stimulant in the Orient. It is being sold as a sexual stimulant all over Asia and regarded as more potent even than Viagra. There has never been an area anywhere in the world with a richer wild life than the savannas of East Africa in the nineteen forties and fifties. In hindsight, I am so grateful that both the VW and we went ashore again in Kenya. Since then the big game life in Africa has gone the same way as the buffaloes in America.

It was at the end of the dry season and we left a thousand feet of dust trail behind us. Time and again we had to stop to allow a herd of elephants to cross the road. We sat over an hour and waited on a thousand zebras and gnus. Here and there under some tree a lion family lazed. Rhinos stood unmoving and just stared at us and giraffes strode around everywhere. To talk about it today is similar to telling a fairy tale. Those days and that environment is gone, likely forever with the exception of pockets of natural parks where the former fauna can be watched "through a looking glass" of predetermined experience.

We were on our way to Amboseli below the Kilimanjaro between Kenya and Tanganyika. We were heading with special government permission to a game reserve where a British film expedition had made the movie *Where no vultures fly* and the Americans later *The Snow On Kilimanjaro*. There were some huts left from the movie days and those were now used for special guests. Responsible for Amboseli Game Reserve was game warden Richard Taberer.

It was a great honor for us to be able to enter Amboseli that had been closed to the public after some bad experiences with visitors. We had left the main road and cruised between the bushes of the dry savannah. There was no road. It took us about half an hour to reach game warden Taberer's bungalow. We felt that he was not too happy to see us. Politely he assigned us one of the huts and a boy. I am sure the boy was not just there to be helping us but to keep an eye on what we did.

The first night in Amboseli is one of the greatest moments in my life. We sat outside this primitive mud hut. A couple of monkeys jumped around in a tree chattering behind us. The sun was sinking, blood red above and behind the mountaintop on the horizon, glittering in the snow. A lion roared somewhere, a rhino snarled and some giraffes strolled majestically in slow motion between the mountain and us.

Taberer was then one of Africa's most respected game wardens. You might well say legendary. He was chosen to guide Queen Elizabeth when she visited East Africa. "Maybe I was a bit lucky that all the animals showed up for Her Majesty," he said.

He had spent thirty years out there among "his animals". He took care of an old rhino that had been hurt in a fight and could not feed itself properly. He left meat with an old rheumatic lion that could not kill any longer. His wife had gotten used to that some animals got more attention than she did. Like Simba for instance (all lions in Africa are called Simba, as you know). He followed Taberer like a dog, a very big and menacing dog I would say, a couple of hundred kilos and ten feet from nose to tail tip. In the evening Simba first rested under the dining table, then at the side of the arm chair and at nights below the bed. He did not like much that others came too close and I can tell you that many did not fancy this lion. When Taberer had to leave for a day or two Simba was sour as hell and all the while guarded the house resting by the door. When Taberer returned they wrestled and rolled around on the veranda.

The lion had been a savior according to Taberer's wife:

"You know, during the Mau Mau uprising many Europeans lived in constant fear for their lives. Simba saw to it that no one bothered us," she said.

After seven years Simba started to disappear for days at a time. Then he was gone for a year. When he showed up Tabererer understood that he wanted him to follow. There out under some trees a little over a mile away, Simba showed off his family, "He wanted to show me why he went away", said Taberer.

Of course being below Kilimanjaro, we had to ask Taberer about Ernest Hemingway. We shouldn't have done that...

"Hemingway was a great disappointment," said Taberer. "A great disappointment. I had admired his writings and saw him as Africa's writer. Now I don't want him back here."

Taberer told how Hemingway with his entourage had neglected the simple rule that in Amboseli the animals count, not the humans. Hemingway just stepped on the gas without any regard for the animals. He just drove right through herds scattering them. He was a big macho kind of guy.

"I will not allow him back here," said Taberer.

Then I showed him a copy of the American magazine Look. It featured Hemingway in Africa with his rifle posing in a picture headlined "The death of a rhino". The trouble, as far as I could see, was that the photo was taken in the Amboseli game reserve where hunting is prohibited. Then there was a photo spread of Hemingway with a couple of "wild" Masai warriors, who had come to him for help to kill a lion that terrorized their village.

"That rhino was never shot," said Taberer. "It died as a result of wounds from a fight. And that the so-called wild Masai warriors would ask an American writer for help to kill a lion is laughable. That wild Masai was a sergeant in the British colonial army fighting in Burma."

We later also paid a short visit to the game park at Murchinson Falls in northern Uganda to get a glimpse of the Blue Nile. We found that the game warden there was not much more appreciative of the writer than Taberer.

"He landed in a small plane on the other side of the river one late afternoon. He never set up camp but slept in the plane and took off the next morning when he felt there were too many crocs in the river to cross it to the station. I just had three little American ladies on a river tour."

I wrote in my book Mara Moja from the Cape to Cape trip that you can do Africa three ways: The sensible way, the hard way or the Hemingway and if you do it the Hemingway no one wants you back. The publisher cut that, because he was also Hemingway's publisher. *Hemingway! Why did you do this to me?*

Bengt started to become weary and said, "let's go home now."

We found there was a ship in Mogadishu, the capital of then Italian Somaliland that could take us to an Italian port. It was just a question of getting on board. We had to get our papers stamped and signed

In Mogadishu more official business was conducted in bars than in offices. It was all a question of finding the bar where you could also find the civil servant who had to sign your papers. It is something special when the head of the immigration police turns to the bartender saying: "Give me the stamp, Giorgio."

It was a bit scary to watch the VW being loaded onto a ship in open sea, as you hear the barge foreman shouting: "OK take it in at the next top of a starboard wave."

They took it. There it was, our old friend dangling over the water to be hoisted in.

How was it the captain in Adrar province of Algeria said it. "Patience is my strength." And it proved also to be our strength in Africa. Could anything ever startle us? We didn't think so at the time.

Heaved on board in a basket we sat at the captain's table for the first decent meal since we presented Cape Towns' mayor with the gift from the mayor of Hammerfest.

We landed somewhere in southeastern Italy. I have never been able to remember all the ports there. The road to Sweden was open ahead. Once again back on these fabulous, European, well-kept roads. It must have felt for our old battered VW similar to what it feels like for a desert walker to creep down between clean sheets after showering off the road dust.

Little did we know that one of the greatest challenges was waiting ahead.

The auto train through the St. Gotthard Pass into Switzerland had left.

"Then let's hit the road," said Bengt. "A bit of snow can't be that bad."

Of course not. We were tuff guys now weren't we? All the sand in Sahara hadn't been able to stop us so we set out. It looked quite all right for a while until the snow piled up on both sides above the windows. No chance to turn around. We struggled on and reached the top and a closed tourist station. Should we turn around and go back to take the train? Or should we continue? We felt that as the road had been plowed so far, it probably was plowed ahead too and to our advantage it was downhill. We saw no signs that the snowplow had turned around. With nose pointing downhill we started our descent. After about a kilometer we found the snowplow but no operator. It was late afternoon so we decided to camp and wait for the driver of the plow to come to work the next morning. As we sat there alone at a campfire on the top of St. Gotthard we felt like kings of the mountain.

No snowplow operator turned up in the morning. We

had to continue downhill because there was no place to turn around. What scared us now was having a snow wall only on the left side of the car. To the right there was nothing but a drop of at least 600 feet. I have never before or after been so scared in my life.

I did not feel my heart in my throat. It had already jumped out.

"I'll walk," said Bengt. "I do not %^@! dare sit in the bus. You at least have some ground on your side."

When he opened the door on the passenger side there was nothing so he ended up crawling over me to get out. For several miles we only had a strip not much wider than the VW to stay on to make it down the mountain. I had my door ajar so I could get out if... Not even today do I want to think about it.

We crept downwards, one nervous foot after the other. Bengt walked ahead of the car and, so to say, felt the road. It was often not so much that we rolled but slid. Several times the right rear tire had half its width in free air.

A trip that under normal conditions might have taken thirty minutes took us nine hours.

When we finally cleared the mountain and rolled into the customs area of the station village, a customs guy advised us that the auto train to Italy would not leave until the next day.

I told him we were not going to Italy, "We are coming FROM Italy." Coming across the pass, I tried to tell him. Impossible," he said. "That pass is not open for automobiles for another six weeks."

I showed our passports with the date stamps.

He took us to the inn to put us on view to the local population.

It was 'Valborgsmässoafton' (Walpurgis Night, April 31) when we rolled into Stockholm, just in time to light the ceremonial bonfire with the family.

GORILLA GORILLA

It was in evenings on Jean de Medina's porch by the Epulu River in the Ituri rain forest that a semi documentary about the mountain gorillas formed in my mind. No one had ever been able to catch them with the camera in the bamboo regions high up in the Ruvenzori Mountains. But it was only after some time at home that I started to work on the project with great help from cinematographer Sven Nykvist who was a close friend of mine. He took enthusiastically to the project. He knew Africa well. His father was one of the first Swedish missionaries in Kongo. He had been to his father's mission stations, he had made a documentary film "Under the Southern Cross" and I had co-written a book with him: *The Journey to Lambarene.*

I was planning a simple nature story about a little boy who admires a hunter and follows him secretly into the jungle while the animals talk to each other about him, until one day he stands in front of a huge mountain gorilla, unafraid and talking to the huge animal.

To that very day no one had ever been able to film the

mountain gorilla (Gorilla Gorilla). Several expeditions had tried without any luck. One traveler who was able to take a few photos of the animal back in the 1930's was Prince Wilhelm of Sweden.

I felt I had a really strong story and presented it to the well-known independent producer, Lorenz Marmstedt of Terra Film in Stockholm. He liked the idea very much and especially that Sven Nykvist would handle the camera.

Sven was already known as Ingmar Bergman's cameraman and during his career he collected two Oscars as cinematographer.

Of course, we did not have the great resources that Hollywood had when they sent Clark Gable and Ava Gardner to Africa to film the movie *Mogambo (1953)*. They set out trying to film the mountain gorillas but had to do the movie with the forest gorillas (Gorilla Berengei) in Gabon, a smaller version of the gorilla. Still, to catch even those apes they built a fence around a couple of gorilla families and added four camera towers. For weeks they collected material, which then could be used in back projections with Clark Gable.

While Mogambo took a crew of 128, I went to Africa with four including myself—Sven Nykvist, Bengt Lindström and a speedway rider, Hasse Björn, to keep our two Land Rovers running and serve as our sound technician.

I remember the day I stepped into the Land Rover/Rolls Royce showroom on Strandvägen by Nybroplan. The sales manager sat comfortably in his room doing crosswords, I suppose. He had been watching me out of the corner of his eye to make sure, I suppose, that I did not make fingerprints on the displayed Rolls Royce. He glanced at me as something the cat had brought in. I went over where he sat in his glass cage and knocked at the door.

"Do you have Land Rovers," I asked.
"Of course, what do you mean, can't you see?"
"Very good, I said, give me two."

Bengt Lindström, Hasse Björn, my wife Lill and I flew one day to Douala in the Cameroon to meet the Land Rovers, all of the supplies and equipment, which would arrive with MS Innaren from Gothenburg. Sven was busy finishing some work at home and would join us in Stanleyville.

It was a hot and humid afternoon of the fifth day at Hotel Akwa Palace and for the sixth consecutive day, we looked for MS Innaren on the harbor list of incoming ships. MS Innaren was shown on the board under the heading of Arriving Shortly. That meant that it could arrive during the night or within a couple of weeks.

I was on the bed under the ceiling fan reading some quasi crime story from the hotel's even quasier supply of bad books. The windows were closed to keep out the street odors. Instead a smell of rancid floor wax slipped in from the corridor. My wife was at the hair salon, not because she needed it, but because she had been told that there were no hairdressers beyond Douala.

The contraption on the nightstand turned out to be a telephone. When it rang it fell off the table by the effort. The shipping agent called to let me know that MS Innaren regretfully was eleven days late.

The next morning the contraption rang again. "I bet," said my wife, "that it is the agent telling you he did not mean eleven days but eleven weeks."

It was indeed the agent who started off to apologize that due to circumstances beyond his control he had been misinformed and in turn misinformed me.

"Monsieur, I am so sorry about not informing you correctly. MS Innaren has arrived. It docked last night!"

As we entered the port area Bengt said: "Did you see the guy at the gate? He had the same type of hat that you bought in Stockholm."

"Maybe PUB has opened a branch down here," said Hasse," because I see a guy over there wearing my shirt." On a box by the cars sat a happy African with a jar of Swedish meatballs he had opened with a screwdriver. We were barely able to prevent him from picking up a tin of Swedish herrings.

It was no use to start an argument about and have it delay our getting out of the port and on to the road. Aware of what had happened also made the customs clear us right away getting rid of a potential problem.

From the last time I was there I knew the road eastward from Douala fairly well via Yaounde and Bouar to Bangui in the Central African Republic. If it had felt like being in a pressure cooker by the coast it now felt more like being in a frying pan. The roads were dust dry and Hasse had to keep his Land Rover a couple of hundred meters behind mine not to be engulfed in my dust tail from the red clay surface. Still when we stopped to see our missionary ladies we could not quite make out if his Rover was green on its way to be red or the other way around.

Where the road forked off to the Swedish church was an old German canon and a cross marking the graves of German soldiers telling you that God and the Kaiser's soldiers came this far but not further in their quest of Cameroon.

We were heading for the ferry outside Bangui, capital of the Central African Republic and a wonder of the art of French seduction in Africa. You could for instance begin with a gourmet dinner at Club Cercle General Leclerc after an aperitif dansant and then do some late eating, drinking and dancing at Le Night Club. Indeed Bangui was impressive as an African colonial city with cafes, cinemas, fashion shops and beauty salons. However, the country outside Bangui was something the

French did not talk about much. It was a land to which the French had a habit of posting civil servants who for one reason or another caused problems at home. While it was a demotion for a French civil servant or officer to be sent to the colonies it was always different for the British. For a young Englishman with military or civil servant ambitions it was part of his career to serve in the colonies.

We saw Bangui at the height of its glory as a French city. There was not much left to see when the former sergeant of the Foreign Legion, sergeant Jean-Bédel Bokassa took over the country, crowned himself emperor in a $20,000 ermine laced robe and began a dictatorship so brutal that it over shadowed the rule of the infamous Idi Amin of Uganda.

It is hard to even imagine the cruelties performed by Emperor Bokassa while still courted by diplomats and the French government. He had a castle in France, an apartment in Paris filled with lovers. For his mistresses in Bangui he built large homes with small lakes in which he kept crocodiles. For lunch entertainment he would throw a prisoner to the crocodiles. On his inaugural dinner he is said to have served human flesh, as a personal kick. Of course, his high-ranking diplomat guests did not know what they were eating. He liked to drive through Bangui in the evening standing in his jeep and randomly shoot people. The French president was his safari guest for big game hunting. His favorite dinner entertainment was torture not just of prisoners but of people he did not like for one reason or another.

We had done our 10,000 miles of grass steppe, forest and bush savanna in just over a week and crossed the river over to Kongo. The border station was as well kept as I remembered it from last time. The customs and immigration officer would not let us go unless we spent the night. His wife insisted on that since she had not talked to a white woman in almost a year and wasn't likely to see any for many more months, at some distant point when her husband had a long home leave.

So we hit the rain forest on familiar roads to Stanleyville. It looked the same; the only change was that it had a couple of more big buildings and bungalows. The Belgians are much like the Swedes, a rather boring but efficient bunch. We bought our provisions and waited for Sven Nykvist. We designated Hasse Björn to handle Martine de Smet who ran Sabena's office at the airport. She was a key person for our film shipments. She was a real looker too so Hasse had no problems except he never got to bed until late at night because Martine was also a musician and led a female jazz band that she had imported from Brussels. The band played at the dining area of the Sabena Guest House. She sang so you could hear it across the Kongo River. She soon became a key person for us. If we needed an auto part, cable Martine. When we needed a tire, cable Martine. In need of money, cable Martine and if any of our several permits expired, cable Martine.

Sven arrived after a few days and we hit the rain forest road that Bengt and I had worn our tires on.
The first white man to cross the Ituri forest was Stanley. It took him exactly 365 days when he was in Africa to rescue another person, who did not want to be saved, Emin Pasha, who camped in Mambasa close to Medina's okapi station.

We headquartered at Medina's camp during almost half of our time in Kongo. We went to work with enthusiasm, happy to have found two Africans to guide us through the camera adventure.

Mambasa was our first camera stop about five miles from our camp at Medina's. There were four Belgians running a territory almost the size of a large country with over 20,000 Africans. The administrator Monsieur

Kampiniere ran the whole area with one cashier, one police assistant and the chief of the prison. So I wondered how that could work. When I asked him how four people could run the area, Kampiniere answered:

"I hire them. The cashier pays them. They spend the money on booze, get drunk so my police assistant arrests them and the prison chief locks them up."

They called it Rotation Kampiniere.

Medina now had seventeen work elephants and over thirty okapis ready for zoos around the world. He had reached the official retirement age and the army wanted to retire him. But the army could find no one qualified to run the station. Also, Medina himself had no roots anywhere. He belonged to the forest. He had become a remarkable person not just as a hunter but also as a mulatto who had broken Kongo's rigid racial system's extreme prejudice. He had sat at the governor's table with his black wife. Could you believe it?

I spent some time at Patrick Putnam's abandoned camp to see if and how I could use it in the film. As late as 1990 I had a letter from Jean Mark, research associate of anthropology at Harvard who was working on a biography on Patrick Putnam. After having read a couple of my books he wanted to hear more about my meetings with Putnam before he died. Putnam had quite a name among anthropologists researching the links to primitive people. I also had letters from Robert Bailey of the University of California.

None of these two researchers knew about Jean de Medina or a young Belgian, Jean David, who was his second in command for many years. When they visited Ituri in connection with Putnam and the pygmies they found some traces of Putnam's camp and heard rumors of some tame elephants. By the Epulu River they found some rusty overgrown ruins on the other side of the road. It was most likely remains of Monsieur David's bamboo motel.

Medina's African foreman, Pascal, eventually took over Medina's job in 1963. A couple of years later, I think it was in 1966, when the Simba rebels terrorized eastern Kongo - much as they do today under various war lords - Medina, his wife and nine children were murdered, the elephants were shot for the ivory and the okapis were slaughtered for food. *

We had found our "actors", the native hunter and his admirer, the little boy who follows him talking to the animals. With Sven Nykvist's photo it was going to be a fabulous saga like composition.

Then lightning struck. The producer, Lorentz Marmstedt, had found a girl friend that he wanted to promote and make into a star. Here was an opening for her.

"Lars, you've sent home some great stuff, but I don't think people can sit and look at black faces for two hours."

He sent me a new script featuring his girlfriend Gio Petré as a female reporter meeting a white hunter played by a French actor George Gallay. It was suddenly a Swedish-French production. Sven and I were upset. We had sent home some of the finest and most artistic and, let me add, charming footage that ever had come

*Footnote: *In 2005 I was informed by the big Oak Ridge breeding station for endangered species outside Jacksonville in Florida that it had opened a camp for the preservation of the okapi by the Epulu River at the very same spot where Jean de Medina had his camp. Dr. Lucas, head of Oak Ridge, and his crew had never heard about Medina and were amazed when I met and told them about Medina and how he had saved the okapi from extinction. The rebels that killed Rivera also killed most of the Epulu population, leaving no one old enough to remember. Oak Ridge station by Epulu was built on the old camp.*

out of Africa. But the new story line was an epitome of banality.

Sven did not say "I don't do crap like that" because he did not use that kind of language. But he went back to Sweden and left Bengt with the cinemascope outfit. Yes, we were making it in cinemascope, the first Swedish film of the wide screen.

Gio was young. So young that her mother sent me a telegram and asked me and my wife to take care of and protect her little girl. The only problem was that my wife had just returned home to the children. Hasse and Bengt now told me about my moral duties as a "body guard". This French guy Gallay had to be watched. He was a lady's man and played his tricks on her. I mean I thought I knew his type and I told him so when she came rushing to me after a take and cried about how he had bitten her lip and fumbled under her dress. Poor girl. I told her it would never happen again. George just laughed it off and said: "Okay, but you'll be surprised."

And sure I got a surprise two weeks of guarding later. The producer, Lorenz Marmstedt, arrived to see what we were up to. He just took his bags to Gio's room and stayed there for a week. After that I figured that she really was fully capable of guarding herself. It should be added that apparently Monsieur Marmstedt had honest intentions. He married Gio later in Sweden.

We were anxious to finish the story, which was leading to the film's climax - the meeting with the mountain gorillas in the bamboo forests of the Ruvenzori range. It was pure camera work so we sent Gio and George Gallay home. We could fit them in later via back projection.

When we headed for the mountains at an elevation of 5-6,000 feet around the village of Lubero we did not have an inkling of how to go about filming the gorillas up there in the bamboo forest. None took us seriously. Especially not the area administrator.

It did not matter to him that I had the special permit from the colonial office suggesting that any local authority should facilitate our work, Captain Rene Wouters in Lubero flatly denied us to risk our lives in the mountains without weapons, which the colonial office denied us to carry. It was a real Catch 22. Finally he agreed to let us go up there in the gorilla mountains if he was certain that we had some protection. He asked us to talk to a farmer, Jacobus Engelbrecht and make a deal with him who had a weapon's license.

"Tell him to come and see me about going up there to hunt in such a way that he won't hunt more than fifty feet from you."

I have always said that if you follow the law to the letter it will help you to get or do what you want. Thus we went filming fully licensed to do that as long as we carried no arms. Engelbrecht went hunting fully licensed. Officially we had nothing to do with each other except in Captain Wouter's mind.

Lubero was not much more than a motel, the administrator's office, a police station, a post office and a couple of Greek and Portuguese run stores. It was the center of a farm community. The slopes up towards the bamboo-covered mountains were the food store for a large portion of eastern Kongo. Every week trucks left with 20,000 eggs, butter, cheese, vegetables, strawberries and chicken. On the field outside Engelbrecht's house grazed Jersey cattle.

Hotel Lacroix was the center of life for the European farm community. God knows what inspired Madame Lacroix to leave her kitchen in Flanders, Belgium to plant her feet into the fertile soil of eastern Kongo. But here she was with the unconquerable energy of a strong middle-aged woman who decides to run her own business. She turned Hotel Lacroix into the best food place east of Lualaba and west of Zanzibar. She was one of the most colorful in an African world, which had no room for pale faces. She was just as formidable a female whether she ran the kitchen help or drank half a dozen men under the table before toward midnight she walked across the yard to her bedroom, whiskey bottle in hand.

"You can write that I drink and fight like a man, but that I have a heart of gold"

We started by visiting the villages closest to the bamboo belt and after a couple of weeks we had defined what we thought would be the most likely area for local gorillas. We then promised to pay for more accurate information about local gorilla families also taking into account that these animals often cover several miles in quest of food. We finally felt that we had enough information to leave Hotel Lacroix and establish a base camp in the bush. Bamboo over, under and around us.

From the Lake Albert down to Lake Kivu along the mountain ridge there were still a few hundred families of the mountain gorilla living. They have an orderly family life. The parents stay together all their lives and the children often stay close to the parents for twenty years. When one parent dies the other often turns into a sour recluse who takes greater risks than he would have with his family. Some of these loners have been the source of frightening tales of gorillas attacking people and dragging women with them into the forest. All that is of course just tales. When there is a shortage of fresh bamboo it sometimes happens that a gorilla ventures into one of the native fields for food. As the villages have spread up the mountain slopes, they have encroached on the forest that feeds the gorillas.

We had finally spotted two families and a lonely male to an area by the Makoka village. We soon realized that we had hardly a chance to get close enough to the families because they were very alert and moved fast. But the old guy was a bit lazier. He stayed fairly constant within an area where we thought we might be able to catch him with the camera. Almost every morning we found his abandoned night resting place. Sometimes we were so close to him that we could hear him tear through the underbrush. It was as if he purposefully circled us to keep us away from his relatives.

Of course the whole thing was a little ridiculous. Experts on African wild life had tried for years to get close enough to the mountain gorillas to study them and film them with tele lenses. Here we were, a couple of guys from Sweden who did not know hoots about these animals but were still determined to film them in Cinemascope, which meant we had to be less than 40 feet from the animal.

Then one day our mountain guide Tschomba came running and put down his spear only a foot from my shoes.

Bwana, iko hapa makaka ngila kabambi. Kabambi kabissa!

If he is as big as you say then he's bigger than tembo, the elephant. Where is he?

Iko hapa kidogo!

Natives have a bit of a distorted sense about distances. Kidogo could be anywhere from three hundred feet to a three-day walk away.

Tschomba had been out checking the tracks from the previous day when from a hilltop he spotted the old, lone animal munching bamboo shots below him. We figured that he might have food there for four to five hours. We then ought to have time to call out reinforcement from a neighboring village. Chief Makasi in Makoko sent us one hundred men, enough to circle the gorilla.

Our idea was that if the natives banged on drums and shouted the gorilla would try to escape in a direction from which came no noise. So we left an opening of about a hundred and fifty feet, mounted the camera and waited. We were just south of the equator, which we had been passing back and forth for weeks.

Once we had the camera set and ready we signaled the natives to start making noise. We were at almost 10,000 feet, just above the bamboo belt and in a forested area. Suddenly there he was, a black haired giant with a silvery back. No, he did not just step out of the forest. It was more like he pushed it back and he drummed his enormous chest. It was a majestic sight. Then as if he wanted to show us his disrespect he put a hand on the stomach and burped with the sound of a freight train coming to a stop. When he did not scare us he beat his chest again. Still unable to scare us he unleashed a roar. He took a couple of quick steps forward to scare us. That's when one of our bearers lost his nerve and threw a spear that hit the gorilla in the abdomen. Enraged the gorilla rushed at the natives. He tore half the behind off one and grabbed another whom he threw into the bamboos where he died with a stick through his chest. When the animal, bleeding profusely, set out towards Bengt who had been running the camera the whole time, Makasi cried out to Engelbrecht to shoot. Engelbrecht first shot around the feet of the giant and that stopped him. He turned around and disappeared into the forest.

I have never before told what happened thereafter. Engelbrecht and I decided to follow his blood trail. We found him sitting under a tree with hanging arms, and I wanted to cry. This should never have happened to such a marvelous creature. Engelbrecht decided that it would be an act of mercy to kill him. We brought his body back to a catholic mission station for preservation.

Words of our quest about how we had found and filmed Le Grand Garcon went out over Kongo and Uganda. In Mambasa he was close to eight feet tall. In Nia Nia on the road to Stanleyville he was over eight feet and at the Sabena Guest House he had reached close to ten feet in height.

The customs officer at the border between Equatorial Africa and Cameroon asked us on our way back to the port of Douala, if we had heard about this big gorilla.

"I think they had to shoot him before he killed them."

"Who were they?"

"Swiss I believe, a big film expedition with a couple of white hunters. You don't go up in those mountains without protection."

"Yes, we understand it can be risky."

"Risky monsieur? If you knew anything about gorillas you would understand that you might lose your life up in those mountains. So what were you up to in Kongo?"

"Just visiting friends and taking pictures."

Gorilla opened at the Palladium cinema in Stockholm. It played there and around the country for a couple of weeks. It later became one of the most popular Sunday matinee movies for several years.

Five years later I found it advertised on a big poster outside a cinema in Fez in Morocco. My first thought was that someone else had made a gorilla movie, perhaps inspired by us

But the poster read: *Un Film de Lars Henrik Ottoson.*

LARS-HENRIK OTTOSON

OUT OF AFRICA—OUT OF MIND

Africa, south of the Sahara and north of South Africa, is worse off today than it was fifty years ago. Aids, malaria, infectious diseases and starvation kill millions every year in addition to the millions murdered to enhance the territorial power of yet another warlord.

The black African nations exist today, it seems, mainly to feed and enrich military dictators, juntas and warlords. The national banks have pipelines to private accounts in Switzerland. Countries like Kenya and Tanganyika that are marginally functional stumble ahead thanks to coffee growing and tourists who come to look at the wildlife. I.e., the little that remains of it.

Where Bengt and I once had to chase off animals to get into our tent in a game reserve, today's tourist has to use binoculars to see them. In Amboseli Game Reserve at the foot of Kilimanjaro the herds of gnus made the earth shake as they stormed over the savannah. Thousands of zebras grazed everywhere. You saw the long necks of giraffes pointing to heaven. Wherever you looked you saw elephant families. Here and there a couple of rhinoceros lazed. And you only had to come close to a group of shading trees to see a dozing lion family.

For the past decades the curse of Africa has been massive poaching for ivory and the flash and burn clearing of land that then fails to give crops after three or four years as the once rich soil turns to dust. The Swedish government through its SIDA organization spent four billion dollars over twenty years on an agricultural project and a school in Tanganyika (today's Rwanda, Burundi, and Tanzania). It was very successful reaping great harvests every year while schooling hundreds of Africans in crop growing. When SIDA felt that it was time for the local government to take charge of the project lock, stock and barrel - what do you think happened? Those who had worked with SIDA went back home to their villages to flash burn as they had always done before. And as farming destroyed more grassland, even greater areas were eaten up by the growing herds of Masai cattle. Cows equal money to a Masai. That's why he doesn't eat his assets.

When I saw that wonderful movie *Out of Africa* in the early nineties I recognized an area in which I had spent months and knew what was behind every turn of the road. To look at the film it was like watching a land that had lost its soul and its dignity. I could imagine how the movie people had been out collecting some dozen zebras and gnus to liven up the picture. And I bet that they did the shoot of the lion family in the Nairobi zoo.
It was pathetic.

The only area in Africa that still has a sizeable animal population is the Kruger Park in South Africa. But even there the elephant's needs for food are hard to meet.

South Africa has become a popular country in which to show your support for African causes and independence - much thanks to the heroic story about Nelson Mandela, a hero to the world.

"There is no longer apartheid in South Africa and black Africans govern the country," writes Andrew Kenny in the world's oldest weekly, the highly respected

Specatator, in January 2002,

What happened then? Every day in South Africa sees an average of 59 murders, 145 rapes and 752 serious crimes. The latest is rapes of children and virgins, which AIDS infected men believe will cure their illness. Twelve percent of the population has AIDS. Prime minister Mbeki assures that HIV cannot cause AIDS. At the same time the country's chief of police says that there is nothing the police can do to stop the violent crimes in the country.

It is a tragic fact that almost every nation in Africa south of the Sahara was better off as colony than it is as independent nations. The colonials never subjected any population to mass murder like the slaughter of millions in countries like Rwanda Burundi, Nigeria, Mozambique, Angola, Uganda, Somalia, Kongo, Liberia, and on and on. Millions butchered to death, boiled in oil and lit like human torches.

When Africans resort to this type of cruel and barbaric behavior they often turn and blame the imperialistic apartheid system. They even blame it on an educational system during the colonial era that prevented Africans from getting a higher education. But the fact is that there were more schools in colonial times in the bush than there are today. Few teachers dare to work outside the cities as they risk to be killed by bands of roving soldiers who have been taught that intellectuals are the great enemies. (Like it was once in Cambodia and Burma). In Africa Europeans were supposed to act as civilized human beings while on the other hand Africans did not have to meet any particular standards.

Black government is no guaranty for black freedom, writes Kenny and I sit here and think that perhaps the African Americans whose forefathers came to America were luckier than their neighbors who stayed behind. Without forced migration to this country maybe we would never have experienced a Michael Jordan or Muhammad Ali. Or for that matter a President Obama!

One of the most sorrowful chapters in African history is the rise to power by Idi Amin in Uganda. But there were, if I may call them that, Mini-Idis, all over Africa. They were corporals and sergeants from the colonial years who fought for power in countries like Sierra Leone, Ghana, Nigeria, Tchad, Kongo, Congo Brazzaville and the Central African Republic.

The latter was governed by a barbarian who loved to sacrifice humans and to drive through the capital Bangui standing in his jeep shooting people at random along the streets.

I stayed for a short period in Bangui, capital of the Central African Republic or some times called Oubangui Shary. It was then a French trading post to the interior of Africa. On the other side of the river was Belgian Kongo. Contrary to the British who were reluctant to station many Englishmen in the bush except as administrators, the French worked as mechanics, drivers, carpenters, etc. That turned a city like Bangui a darn sight livelier than British colonial towns. Bangui had a big French population with hotels, restaurants, shops etc. After the independence that idyllic spot in Africa soon disappeared.

Of course the Africans had the dream that everything was going to be so much better when they got rid of the colonials, the imperialistic bloodsuckers and the stuck up white folks.

Then, in so many places it turned out so much worse instead. Of course you can dig up many reasons to this as a result of the colonial system. But there is actually only one that has contributed to the unrest more than anything else and that was the way the colonial powers divided up the continent without any regard for tribal areas or fiefdoms. The colonials drew a map on which they looked for natural borders. The borders came to split tribes and package them with other tribes of different language and with different beliefs, traditions and ways of life. The colonialists only saw a lot of black faces – "they all look the same to me." Nowhere in the western world was there any respect for the black man. So if you could enslave him in America, where he learned both to read and write, why should one show him more respect in his primitive homeland? However, even in pre-colonial Africa a native had it better than an early black slave in America. He lived his own life in peace and with dignity in accordance with local African traditions. He and his family were secure within the social structure of the tribe. He had definitely more dignity than the sharecroppers, who slaved in America,

The social difference between a European and an African was of course enormous. But the colonial powers were also anxious to keep peace and village security. The unrest in Africa south of the Sahara began when more and more Africans left the rather peaceful village life and began moving to big cities like Nairobi and Lagos. Cut away from the security of their tribal life they were now thrown into an every day fight to survive in a surrounding and culture entirely foreign to them.

History might look differently at the development in South Africa since it was so different from the colonization of the rest of the black Africa. In the south there was a well-organized Zulu kingdom fighting the British and the Boer settlers the way the American Indians fought the European settlers. Much of the success of South Africa's place among the most important countries in the world stems from the Zulu traditions and its place as the world's gold and diamond treasury.

French, British, Portuguese and Belgians all differed in the way they ran their African colonies. The British were the ones who kept the greatest distance between black and white but at the same time, they trained Africans to run administrative routines as post office clerks, native police constables and lower ranking officers etc. It was part of the career of a British officer to spend some years in the colonies. He might start with a position as district administrator. He soon trained an African ascari to handle paper work in the office and taught someone to run the post office. It freed the British officer to spend more time hunting. The end result of all this was that the British colonies were better equipped than all the others to handle independence. Contributing to the relative stability was also that in countries like Kenya and Uganda European coffee farmers generally remained after independence.

The French did not have much faith in the Africans. They kept all jobs, except the very menial ones, for French workers, down to grease monkey work on the transport trucks. Natives were not encouraged to speak and understand French. The result was that there were a lot more Frenchmen in French colonies than Englishmen in the British colonies.

The Belgians kept the lid on the native population for a long time with some rather strict racial barriers and limiting natives to an education up to what in the U.S. would be fifth grade. The word makaka (monkey) was finally prohibited as the way to address natives. The Belgians allowed Africans to have low clerical jobs and as mechanics. When the Belgian king visited the colony he lifted many of the racial bans like allowing Africans into restaurants.

I was sitting on the Sabena Guest House veranda having a drink when four Africans sat down at a table next to mine. I was surprised to see the waiter take an order. Half an hour later the white bar tender came with their drinks. They dropped the glasses with a scream. He had heated them to burning point. They left right away and

In 'my Africa' there was little or no risk of violence.

the problem was solved to the satisfaction of both white patrons. This attitude helped fuel a hatred in Kongo and that hatred is now channeled to other subjects, just like it used to be over a hundred years ago, before the Belgians, when tribes and villages were in constant feuds. Today, no village is safe from another village, no warlord is safe from another warlord and in a few years almost six million people have been killed in eastern Kongo.

In the Portuguese colonies the discrimination was minimal. The colonials often formed families with native women and never regarded themselves as colonizers but as citizens. At least that was the case in Mozambique until about ten years ago when the mutual tolerance took a fall. The Portuguese colonies were the finest examples in Africa of the transfer from colony to nation.

There were some great unrest and heavy fighting in Angola, much because of the unrest that welled in over the border from Kongo.

I remember that I at one time asked in Lubero about a man who had a store, if he was a white man.

"No bwana, he is not a white man."

"So he is an African?"

"No bwana, he is not an African."

"If he is not white and not African, what is he?"

"He is Portuguese, bwana."

The French never really adjusted as I said before. There was a saying that Frenchmen came to Africa with a suitcase and left with a fully loaded truck.

Of course with the British all was different. Whether in Kenya or Nigeria the British were all jolly good fellows and press on regardless old boy. And I can tell you it was a sight to see them in 42F uniforms all buttoned up in their colonial regalia dancing with wives in soaked satin dresses under a big picture of Her Majesty the Queen.

The English gave a dignity to their colonies that the other countries failed to do as they, at the same time, took an interest in actively contributing to promote the colonies for settlements and tourism. The coffee farms in Kenya produced some of the finest mocha in the world.

Throughout the years I spent in Africa from north to south, east to west I never carried a gun. I have slept in the car by the roadside or parked in some village. Entering Kenya with the VW during the Cape-to-Cape trip we parked for the night behind a big roadside advertising board to protect us from a dust storm. We woke up in the morning, as so often before, with kid faces pressed against the windows. They laughed and with their hands sort of pistol pointing at us saying bang bang. We bang banged back.

Back on the road we stopped to read the sign, it said YOU ARE ENTERING MAU MAU TERRITORY, CHECK YOUR GUN!

THE ANCHOR MAN

Now, how did all this about and my time in Africa end? Except, of course, for what I have already told you. Maybe I could say that it ended in a multiplicity of things, at the time and also later in life.

As one country after another in Africa claimed independence during the late fifties and into the sixties, a need arose for newsworthy information about the events.

Swedish TV's political editor, Henry Christensson, called me a few days after I got back from filming Gorilla. He wanted to know if I, by chance, could talk a little about how I, as a journalist, saw the events in various countries in Africa. As news arrived back to back, so to say, I was soon on TV almost every night. Henry would call and say for instance "Can you give me two and a half minutes Kongo tonight?"

At the time, Olle Björklund was the very popular anchor. However, he fell for the temptation to make a bit of extra money as spokesperson for an encyclopedia. Now, you would think that was a rather dignified subject to promote. But the strict rules of the Swedish state television allowed their employees NO outside commercial activities and promotions. Björklund was fired the same day and when I came in for the briefing Åke Söderqvist, then head of the Aktuellt News Hour, was in a bind, he had no anchor.

"Lars, do you think you can read the news tonight?"

"Sure, why not," I said.

That he asked me was perhaps not so surprising as he knew about my years as a reporter and commentator with the BBC Swedish section in London. When later a new weekly magazine FIB Aktuellt put me on the cover of its first issue I was crowned Mr. Aktuellt. It was at the same time as Kongo split from Belgium. But before the country had a nation wide accepted government - which by the way it does not have to this day after fifty years - the United Nations took over for a while. Sweden contributed with the first UN battalion. As administrator UN appointed an old friend of mine, Sture Linnér, who arrived in Leopoldville after heading a Swedish mining company in Liberia.

One of my first jobs as anchor was to go back to Kongo to report on the Swedish U.N. battalion. I actually arrived there several days ahead of the military. When the Swedish soldiers jumped out of the huge transport planes ready to tackle an enemy, I stood there with a mike and said:

"Hello guys, welcome to Kongo."

In the capital of Kinshasa the troops fanned out and Sture Linnér established his administration at a hotel. Isolated from the rest of the country and not having a clue what happened out there he asked me if I would dare to fly up to Kishangani (Stanleyville) and check the situation there. If I would risk it he would send a couple of soldiers with me. I told him that I would go there, but without any soldiers. The Africans would not know the difference between a Swedish U.N. uniform and a Belgian, which they hated. But I would not mind a couple of civilian guys.

We landed with a small plane without intermezzo and found the place surprisingly peaceful. Kinshasa was the town where Patrice Lumumba had been a post office clerk. His presence before he headed for Kishangani and the job as the country's first president apparently had a calming influence on the population in Kishangani. I was met with the tragic message that a rebellious group that called itself Simba had murdered Jean de Medina and his family. Simba was led by a corporal from the old colonial army. It was said that they had thrown Medina's body in the river to feed the crocodiles.

At the end of 2008 the memories of my U.N. trip to Kongo came to life as Sweden was sending another battalion to Africa, to the Republic of Tchad to guard the Darfur refugee camps. On the day that the Swedish troop left home, TV's Aktuellt played my old tapes from Kongo as a reminder of Sweden's previous U.N. involvement in Africa.

It did not take Swedish TV long to send me out again. This time to Cuba where the placement of Russian missiles called out the U.S. Navy to a blockade of Castro's island. The world trembled fearing another world war. Sweden at the time was one of the few non-aligned countries with Cuban contacts, and the only country that might have a chance to get a reporter into Cuba. To get a report from inside Cuba would be a world scoop.

Swedish TV negotiated with the Cubans who hoped that a Swedish report might give the western world a more positive impression of "Castro land". Sweden did not belong to NATO and had a left leaning government at the time.

I remember being met on my way into the Aktuellt office by a flustered Åle Söderqvist. He put some documents in front of me to sign.

"Why the hell am I going to sign a life insurance?"

"Because you are going to Cuba, They are holding the

SAS plane to Prague at the airport for you. Your camera man is on board and your wife is on her way there with your travel bag under police escort."

My cameraman was Roland Palm, yes, the same man I had spent some chilly nights with a few years earlier while driving south from North Cape. There wasn't an empty seat on the plane so we had to sit crammed into the cockpit.

Aktuellt had worked for weeks to get a permit to get into Cuba. The key to get in was kept in Prague. After a night in the Czechoslovakian capital in company with a group of heavy drinking communist dignitaries, a Russian plane waited to take us to Castro. We had to fly via Newfoundland where I had been once before. Gander airport had not changed a bit. The piano that Sixten Ehrling used to accompany Jussi Björling that unforgettable day was still there but out of tune. This time it was not de-icing that delayed us but defecting.

A group of Czechoslovakian special workers refused to board the plane again and demanded asylum. It created a never-ending scream fest when the party "politruks" tried to force the men onto the plane. The Canadians said regardless of the outcome they would not let the plane take off until diplomats had come from the Czechoslovakian embassy. We were finally flagged off minus the defectors. The politruks kept cursing on the plane. It probably had to do with who was to blame for bringing the defectors on board in the first place.

Roland and I expected to be warmly welcomed to Cuba and shown all sorts of favors. But we did not more than get off the plane before we were arrested and deposited in jail. And I can tell you there are better places to spend a weekend than in a Castro jail.

It took some time for us to grasp the situation. Finally we understood that Swedish TV - or perhaps it was Åke Söderqvist - had sold whatever Roland and I could produce to the BBC in London and CBS in the United States. Whatever we could produce would be the world scoop of the year. I don't know how the Cubans got wind of any deal with BBC and CBS but they sure did not like it.

When the interrogators realized that Roland and I were not part of any deal or conspiracy to assassinate Fidel, they moved us to house arrest at a hotel in Havana close to the harbor. Cuba did not have many friends in the world so they decided to go easy on friendly Swedes. The Swedish Foreign Office (UD) had its finger in that. Sweden had no representation in Cuba so UD called for Ambassador Dryselius from the Swedish embassy in Venezuela to go to Cuba and get us out of the jam. What surprised us was that no one tried to stop Roland from taking pictures and filming. Then Dryselius explained that the Cubans would not worry about that because at the airport they would walk us through a magnetic gate that would erase anything and everything we might have filmed.

To get good harbor shots and reel in the silhouettes of the blockading US Navy Roland had to hang so far outside the window that we tied a sheet between his ankles and the bedpost.

Ambassador Dryselius had brought his wife and they moved into a room next to ours. Mrs. Dryselius borrowed some pots and pans and supplies from the Norwegian consulate. The smell of newly baked bread and pancakes traveled down the corridor but the female guards placed to watch us with their Russian AK rifles sternly refused any capitalistic bread bribe. Some of them were really quite cute.

In the meantime at home in Sweden the newspaper headlines screamed '**TV-OTTOSON DISAPPEARED IN CUBA!**'

Dryselius could not do much communicating because Castro had put a Swedish communist, Alan Pettersson as PBX operator who did not allow any calls through to Sweden.

I told Roland not to use the total 16 mm length in a cassette, only about half. I did not want all the eggs in one basket. I was going to ask the ambassador to walk through the non-erasing diplomatic gate at the airport with one or two reels as Roland and I walked through the eraser with the rest to the full satisfaction of the Cuban officials. A good plan, I felt. Except, of course, that I had not discussed it with Dryselius.

It took some doing to convince the ambassador to help us. I asked him to also get onto the plane to make sure that we were safely on board. Then all he had to do was to stand by the seat under which he had put the reels. He did it!

There was a big ballyhoo reception for us arriving in Copenhagen because the Russians for some reason did not want to land at Arlanda airport in Stockholm. Our footage was now showing around the world and I presume Swedish TV (or Söderqvist) made some good money.

When I asked Söderqvist why he sent me to Cuba and not one of the regular staff members he said:

"Lars, I could have gotten anyone of them into Cuba. But I knew only one guy I was certain to come back out and bring a story."

I took that as a compliment.

I kept freelancing with Swedish Television for several years. A couple of things however, started to rock the boat - fed by that (in-) famous Swedish jealousy. One was that a magazine appointed me the best-dressed man in Sweden. The other was that I drove a Mercedes Benz, which I actually had bought for a decent price from the American Ambassador when he was transferred.

In a basically homogenous and truly social democratic country where all are equal you should not stand out.

You should blend in. Exceptions are only allowed for rock stars and athletes.

I admit that I dressed better than most of my colleagues. Jacket, tie, cuffs, and vests with brass buttons and in contrasting colors like red or yellow. And I kept my hair neat. Another problem came from the fact that I had no party book, which you needed at the time if you intended to climb the state controlled ladder at Swedish public TV.

When I was in Chicago with Ingemar Johansson to watch the fight between Muhammad Ali and Sonny Liston, I received a cable from Åke Söderqvist informing me that I was fired. I had been in his office two days before and resent the fact that although he knew it then, he did not have the guts to tell me.

On the other hand, I came to later value the event itself because it allowed me to expand my business. Also, a new people's wave called for a more democratic looking guy in sports shirts and unkempt hair. Not my cup of tea at the time.

Before too long The Ottoson Group of Companies contained an advertising and PR agency, Ottoson Production, an expo company, Ottoson Display and a trading company, Ottoson Trading. The ad agency ran campaigns for Esso (Exxon), Volkswagen, Peugeot, Libra stockings, Separator, Scania Vabis trucks etc. I created some slogans that still count big such as 'Ha alltid Esso i tankarna'- Always keep Esso in the tanks (which makes sense only in Swedish where 'tanks' in Swedish is the same word as 'thoughts'). The display company built exhibits at trade fairs around the world for Stora Kopparberg - the world's oldest corporation and several others. It also handled the Christmas decorations on the five main shopping streets and strolls in Stockholm. The trading company was a search engine for smaller Swedish companies seeking international contacts.

The Ottoson Group had 55 employees in the office at Gamla Brogatan 32 (Old Bridge Street) in Klara, the classic commercial and artistic center of Stockholm. One of our largest customers was a pioneering company in the world' growing dialysis industry. My son Peter, as an art director had worked for months on a catalogue and visuals.

One day the company head, Anders Althin Sr., and I stood in my office when Anders says:

"Only one thing left. What do we call the company?"

As he looks out the window from the third floor he sees a small medical supply store and above it the street sign Gamla Brogatan. GAMla BROgatan,

"Hey, let's call it Gambro!"

Gambro is world leading today on dialysis equipment. The only real competition they have had came from the son of Anders Ahltin Jr., who succeeded his father as Gambro president and quit when the company was taken over by a conglomerate. He moved to Florida, started Althin Medical in Miami twenty years ago and soon gave Gambro a match all over the world.

I felt good in the old area bordering Hötorget with the Konserthuset, the Concert House where musicians once a year give room for the Nobel Laureates. I felt at home in this part of town where artists met at taverns surrounding the three daily papers. That's where I started my career writing for ten öre a line. It was here at the restaurant Tysta Mari that Sweden's national poet Nils Ferlin wrote some of his most memorable poems on the back of menues. They just about paid for a bite and a beer. And a bit more for the waiter if he could sell it to a newspaper,

Ottoson Display had built exhibits for Sandviken in Sao Paolo and Tokyo and for Stora Kopparberg in Leipzig and Barcelona. Now the state sponsored Swedish Export Association gave us the job to build a Swedish pavilion for 26 companies at the International Trade Fair in Chicago. It went fairly well and I kept a Swedish service office in Chicago for a while, but closed it when the manager took off with the money.

What old friends remember from the big Chicago fair is that I was invited to a very popular TV talk show together with the mayor and the governor. Those were the days when svenska flicka was synonymous with sexual habits of Swedish girls. I expected that the subject would come up and was prepared for it. When the host, after we had debated morals for a while, asked me if I would approve of my teenage daughter going to bed with a boy, I answered:

"The way you put it, going to bed, indicates to me that they are indoors in close proximity to the hygiene of a bathroom. I think that is definitely preferable to their doing it in the back seat of a car at a drive in."

The camera skipped me and I was not asked another question or invited back into the debate about world morals.

When I started the Ottoson Group I had a partner, Robert Turner, one of the finest graphic artists and illustrators of all time in Sweden. I guess I was more smitten by work than he was. He constantly complained about too much work saying do we really need to have so many customers? "No, I said, but if you want to change that old Volkswagen to something more reliable you'd better work." He replied one day:

"Aren't you the guy who coined the slogan 'No one yet knows how old a Volkswagen can get?'"

Of course I was, but that did not mean that I had to adhere to what I got paid to say.

Others took it literally so later Robert took his sketchpad and old Volkswagen and moved to the small idyllic town of Simrishamn on the east coast of Skåne. He was still driving that Volkswagen six years later.

It was a hectic time that never allowed time to stay still. My wife Lill was taking care of bookkeeping and finances. She was a CPA and kept a tight grip on the money. It left me free to do what I was supposed to do, bringing in the money, not bookkeeping it.

This was during the years when banks were still banks run by people and not by computers or computer enhanced individuals employed for robotic services.

Thinking back on how banks became involved in your business seems almost unreal today. As an ad agency we had to pay the newspapers within a stipulated time to keep the authorization to receive ad commissions. I had to pay on time but my customers often did not. And the largest ones such as SAS and Esso were the worst. If I came into the bank on the first weekday of a month, the bank director would look at me and say "and how much do you need today?" We are talking about a hundred thousand kronor or more. When I asked him once how he could do this just on a bank draft he told me that he knew how hard my wife and I worked and had no intention to fail us when in need of assistance. That's how things used to work in Sweden. I don't know how it worked over here where so many banks feature the word trust in their names.

My wife Lill suffered from the same misconception often found among administrative staff, namely that sales people are a pain in the butt. They spend too much on the road, they forget to enclose receipts or verify expenses. I used to tell my wife that I did not give a hoot about some missing receipt as long as a guy made sales. I told her staff too that they were a cost item while the sales person was an asset.

It used to surprise my customers that for a promotional campaign I did not first talk about it with the client's management but with the sales people on the floor or on the road. They, after all, were the ones who really knew what their customers were buying and it was they who needed "ammunition."

The Association of Swedish Advertising Agencies (Annonsbyrå Föreningen, AF) held the authorization to work as an ad agency, key to the 15 percent commission from newspaper advertising. It resulted in a lot of money if you were, for instance, running a national campaign for Volkswagen. The ad agency could in a case like this afford to give away the artwork free. But with the small advertiser, in need of a one page ad in a technical magazine for a couple of hundred you had to charge for the artwork and copy involved. Many times an ad in a business-to-business magazine craved more product knowledge than a screaming copy and ad for ladies' stockings.

I felt that the system was wrong. An agency should be able to get paid for its work and not rely on commissions. So I started to bill our work and return the 15% commissions to the clients. They liked it. But the big agencies, such as Ervaco, and J. Walter Thompson did not. If they were just going to get paid for work alone, they would have to cut activities like test kitchens and contact people who were basically nothing more than messengers between the client and the art directors and copy writers, who in my opinion should be the ones working with the clients without a middle man.

Together with two other agencies I formed SARF (The Swedish Advertising and Promotional Association). It grew in membership and in a year had surpassed the old association in membership. In the U.S., the ad industry's paper, Advertising Age, headlined an article: Does the Future come from Sweden?

SARF with me as chairman became the association for the creative people in the advertising business. When even the largest customers defected the big agency association, AF folded and Sweden was written up in Adverting Age as the first country to use the non-commis-

The oldest villa in Stockholm's Djursholm, built in 1894.

sion system. The magazine called me a pioneer.

The formation of SARF also led to the establishment of several small creative agencies and it gave new opportunities for the single artist. All those creative people who earlier had to work in the big agency system could now work directly with the advertiser, being paid by the advertiser and not by some agency.

The years that I led SARF we were sued by the AF and the newspapers, which had their hands in each other's pockets, for competition interference. They lost after having run the trade for over 30 years.

I see SARF as my professional contribution to the Swedish advertising industry.

'THE CHAMP' AND ABBA

I think people remember me best, that is, those who are not dead by now, as the voice that came over the radio and gave them the unforgettable fight report describing Ingemar "Ingo" Johansson winning the heavy weight championship of the world on June 29, 1959 at the Polo Grounds in New York. In Sweden it was 3.59 in the morning when Floyd Paterson was decked by "Thor's Hammer". At home Swedes went ballistic.

Swedish Radio could not broadcast the fight for moral reasons deeming boxing an immoral and inhuman sport. Thus, they refused the greatest event in Swedish sports history. The Philips Company scooped the biggest PR event ever by leasing the popular Radio Luxembourg broadcasting station for a couple of nights.

Outside of Swedish Radio there were not many reporters who could cover a sports event. As a matter of fact I believe I was the only one. I knew boxing from my time writing about it at Nya Dagligt Allehanda and I commented on many Swedish fighters who fought in England during my BBC sojourn.

To help me at the ringside I had the *Göteborgs Posten* sports editor Lennart Crusner who knew Ingemar since he was an aspiring local boxer in Gothenburg (Göteborg). In Stockholm, to keep the listeners company and entertained before and after, was my old friend Pecka Langer. This eminent writer and entertainer and I spent many late dinners at Stora Hotellet in Norrköping when I worked at the conservative daily and he worked at the social democratic one.

We used a week before the fight for testing the airwaves and help the Swedes to find the station on the scale. I reported from the training camp up at Catskills in the hills north of New York City or by grabbing people on the street with my microphone asking what they thought about the fight. Pecka kept talking from the studio in Stockholm.

I carried a small tape recorder, about the size of a shoebox, and of the kind that was used by most radio stations in Europe. But I was not in Europe. I was in the USA and dealing with ABC to handle the transmission to Luxembourg.

When I turned up at the ABC with my tapes it was like an icy wind swept through the corridors. Non-Union tapes! Are you crazy, man? No one at ABC dared to touch them. So instead of my little recorder hanging from my shoulder, I found myself with a recording van and a couple of "helpers" - one to carry the recorder, one to carry the mike and a producer to oversee everything.

Returning with proper union approved tapes I sat down to edit them. But I was not supposed to do that either. It had to be done by a tape slicer guided by an editor and a producer. Now, the problem was that they did not have a clue what the tapes with my Swedish comments and translations were all about. I had no use for the technicians but I sure had to pay them. As I worked at the splicing table I basically paid four guys to play cards and have coffee. Of course I did not have to worry about the costs, which were none of my business.

But my business was for this fight to happen and it

New York June 26, 1959. The new Heavy Weight Champ celebrates. L-R: Harokd Kosell, "Whitey" Blumstein, Ingo, Edwin Ahlquist and Lars Henrik.

was darn close that Philips in Stockholm would cancel if the unions did not give a little. Here I was, a Swede capable of understanding the need for unions to protect workers rights but foreign to a union system that made four jobs out of one.

It was obvious from the start that the odds for the fight were heavily in Paterson's favor.
But, of course, people wondered a bit about this knock out punch called Thor's Hammer. Would it hit again? Like it did a couple of months earlier in Gothenburg?

The American heavy weight challenger Eddie Machen had come to the city to dispose of this Swedish boxer before he took on the world champion Floyd Paterson. This Gothenburg event was just a formality. Indeed, it became sort of a formality - but headlined by Ingemar Johansson. Machen took a ten count in the first minute of the first round and that elevated Ingemar to the status of challenger.

Ingemar was not the first Swede in a U.S. heavy weight ring. The first was Harry Persson, enormously popular in Sweden in the late twenties. He arrived in New York, "just like any other European boxer" to be prey in an American ring. Soon promoters realized that if they did not stop him he might take the title to Europe. So in a fight for the right to meet the champion and as the match unfolded the promoters realized that Harry might win, so he had to be stopped. The promoters did it by hissing up the trunks on his opponent and then disqualify Harry for low blows. Years later two Swedish heavy weights, John Andersson and Olle Tandberg won several fights in the United States. Olle Tandberg, the house painter from Skarpnäck, was awarded an elimination fight for a shot at the heavy weight title against the number one ranked challenger Jersey Joe Walcott. The fight took place at Stockholm's old Olympic Stadium in 1947. Tandberg lost on points. Jersey Joe Walcott became the world heavy champion in his next fight.

Edwin Ahlquist, one of the most respected figures in Swedish sport, managed Ingemar Johansson. With Ingemar - who, by the way, never liked to be called Ingo – came, as sparring partner, Europe's at the time best light heavy weight, Lennart Risberg.

As the American sports journalists watched Ingemar train noticing his discipline and, conviction and positive attitude, they started to upgrade him. He was also in many other respects so different to any heavyweight they had ever seen. He was polite and rather quiet, never bragged and was not surrounded by a bunch of hangers on that they were used to see with top ranked fighters. Instead his family surrounded him. There was a lot of talk about Ingo training on a diet of his mother's meatballs. And the fact is she did indeed cook a lot for him.

We all know what happened two minutes and three seconds into the third round. Thor's Hammer struck and a guy from Gothenburg was heavyweight champion of the world.

There at ringside was Elizabeth Taylor holding mamma Johansson's hand. There was Gary Cooper and Errol Flynn who after the fight followed Ingo into the shower in his tuxedo. Errol had been quite a good prizefighter once.

No radio reporter or personality then or thereafter to this day has had as many listeners in Sweden as I had that night. At four a clock in the morning when the fight ended Sweden was intoxicated by joy. My wife, taking a 10-mile taxi ride home from friends, was not allowed to pay the fare when the driver realized who she was.

Many Swedes have reached world status as athletes, but no one can match the fame of Ingemar. We have had Björn Borg in tennis, the skier Ingemar Stenmark, hockey player Sven Tumba... Ingemar Johansson, the heavy weight champion, was special because from pampas in Argentine to mining towns in Africa or in Tibet they have no clue about tennis stars, skiers or runners - but they sure knew who was the heavy weight champion of the world. Every little kid in the slummy projects of New York and Detroit knew his name. Okay, perhaps not as much now as when Ingemar was champion. He was the one and only heavy weight champion before inflation hit the sport. Today five professional boxing bodies, each with seventeen weight classes, have a champion. In other words there are five heavy weight champs. From eight champions in eight weight classes today's boxing world has 73 champions all categories. Also, Ingemar was the last European and the last white champion.

Since the organization of the world of pugilism in 1890 when John L Sullivan became the first recognized world heavy weight champion, there had only been 20 champions. Ingemar Johansson became the 21st. His name is up there with Jack Dempsey, Joe Louis, Rocky Marciano. He was only the third European to be champion following Primo Carnera and Max Schmeling.

Ingemar lost the return a year later against Floyd Paterson in the fifth round. I suppose the first fight had been a bit too easy and maybe - I say only maybe - he had not prepared himself with the same intensity as he did for the first fight. The third fight in Miami in 1961 was a gruel piece of boxing. It could have gone either way. Both Ingo and Floyd were stone tired. They staggered around the ring and it was only a question of who was going to "knee" first. It was Ingo in the sixth round.

Among sport greats there is no one I have admired more than Ingemar. I got to know him well right after the first fight. We did a speaking job together on the film from the fight. It was showing every hour of the day in cinemas all across Sweden. At Rigoletto in Stockholm it ran from ten in the morning until after midnight. Then, we toured the country with our "show". Following a first appearance at the Gröna Lund amusement park in Stockholm in front of 20,000 screamers we fanned out into the country.

Ingemar of course made a lot of money, but he also lost a lot, mainly to some friends he trusted and whom he had let handle some of his affairs like accountants and auditors. In his honesty he could not imagine that pals he had known all his life could ensnare him in worthless projects and cheat him out of money. He was true to his family and his parents were close to him for as long as they lived. Over in the U.S. they stayed for months with him during the winter. This kind of family closeness, which is common in America, is unusual in Sweden, I am sorry to say.

What Ingemar never got over were the Swedish tax collectors. He had made his money in the U.S. and paid his taxes there. Still, for almost thirty years he could not land in Sweden without being taken into a room at the airport and asked how he intended to pay his taxes. For years they harassed him in spite of the double tax agreement between Sweden and the U.S. that you pay taxes where you earn the money.

We came to be neighbors in America, even lived on the same street in a small town called Lighthouse Point north of Fort Lauderdale and Pompano Beach. One day in 1971 I came with my cart in an aisle at the Publix super market and bumped into Ingemar's cart. He had been living, or tried to live, in many places from Switzerland to California during the winters until he found this peaceful oasis on the Florida east coast and bought a house. I lived just down the street after taking over the running of a weekly paper in the neighborhood.

Lighthouse Point had maybe 3,000 inhabitants. It was a small villa place surrounded by the city of Pompano Beach.

Ingemar and I had moved to the same little town and to the same street in the same week. We stayed neighbors for many years until Ingemar bought a small motel on the A1A beach boulevard in Pompano about a mile away. After some years he sold that too and moved with his family to an apartment in Lighthouse Point, close to the Intracoastal Waterway.

I often wondered how this man who had made a living hitting guys unconscious could present this picture of middle class cameral peace, who golfed with the chief of police and the doctor and had early morning coffee when the city merchants and officials met at Kiwani's Coffee Klatches at 6 a.m.

I raised the subject with him one day and he said he had two sorts of friends - good ones and less good ones. "Good ones are like you. Less good ones are a couple of dudes I rumble with now and then in the Bahamas for a couple of party days to sort of loosen up and then return to my good friends."

Ingemar was the celebrity of Lighthouse Point and

Pompano Beach. Wherever you were in the city with Ingemar it was "Hi Champ" or as the Chief of police said: "We are mighty proud to have Ingemar Johansson as a Pompano Beach resident. In every respect he is a champion."

Without doubt Ingo was the most famous entity in town. The other was a balloon, the Good Year blimp that showed up on TV during major sports events. One of the great promotional pictures taken for the city was Ingemar stepping out from the Blimp.

When Ingemar's family was in town visiting they often complained that he did not cut the grass, answer the phone or pay the bills.

"Why on earth don't you do that?" I asked

"I always do when I'm alone and not told," he said.

I can vouch for that.

Ingo became an avid golfer. His putting was perhaps not the greatest but he seldom had to use more than two shots to reach the green. The members of the Pompano Beach Golf Club wondered how come he played in an old pair of sneakers. He said: "Why should I dress better than I play?"

Back to life in Stockholm in the early 1960s: When the family moved to a new house in Djursholm in 1962 with a view of the Stockholm archipelago from our house high up on the top of a hill, the Ottoson Group was running at full speed in every way.

The leading Swedish pop band was Hep Stars followed by Fabulous Four. Both of them had grave tax problems. I don't know who came up with the idea for them to come to me with the problem. I think it was their record producer Stickan Andersson.

Consequently the Hep Stars gang turned up in Djursholm one day. Two Thunderbirds came roaring up hill to the house. In, with shoulder length hair and Afghan coats walked five Hep Stars. My mother, the old musical diva, almost fell over when she saw this wild bunch.

The lead music writer in the group, Benny Andersson, asked me if I could help them to stabilize the situation with the Swedish tax authorities. I represented a combination of celebrity, TV anchor and was familiar with the entertainment world plus, I was married to an active CPA.

The situation was really bad. The boys (they were not much more) owed more than a million kronor, which in those days equaled about $200,000 in back, taxes.

When I asked what they did with the money they received from a concert they just said they divided the gate cash between them.

"Do you have any now?"

"There might be some in my car," said Benny

There, in the trunk were 50,000 kronor in a shoebox! It had been there for some time, as I found out, as payment from a concert about a week ago. The trunk was not locked.

Benny Andersson was probably the only one who understood the situation while the others were in total orbit when it came to money obligations.

We never wrote a formal contract. In that particular area of business a contract is generally a 100-page nightmare. The music industry is among the pets of international law firms and would have taken weeks to formulate.

I simply let them sign an obligation to let me collect their gate money from concerts etc. and in turn would pay 50% to the tax collector, give each group member 75 kronor a day towards living expenses and escrow the rest for a rainy day.

You can't believe how they cried over the seventy-five a day. It just about "rubbed out the chicks."

Many times regular parks could not handle all of the fans. Then sports stadiums and racetracks had to be used. On such occasions I dispatched my son Lars who stood at 6'5" and is built like a wrestler to collect. No one ever argued with him.

The other group we handled was Fabulous Four. They were a pretty good and popular band, but never reached the fan status of Hep Stars grouped around master musician Benny Andersson. He came from a home of music. Both his parents were musicians and he was schooled in the classics. While almost all pop bands in the world relied on guitars and some times a keyboard, which made for a lot of what I call Schrammel Music, Benny early on used a range of instruments for enhancement, including violins.

When Swedish rock bands wanted to do a recording they went to studios in London and worked with back up musicians. On a stage, hopping around, and screaming a tune with equally screaming fans, it does not matter how you sound, as everyone loves you for the way you jump around and riff it or try to anyway. If you can hold two accords and jump you have it made if you ask me. At an open-air concert no one pays much attention to how your music sounds, only to how you move. But when it comes to making a record there's no stage appearance to rely on. So when Hep Stars went to London to make a record Benny could chose among the back up musicians who sit there every day hoping to make some money with a recording band.

Our children thought it was pretty salt, as they put it in the lingo of that day – today they would have said cool - to have parents who knew more about pop music and band members than their friends. My knowledge of the pop industry came from listening on the radio to programs like Top Ten etc. Every step up or down on that ladder involved money gained or lost.

Then one day in the spring of 1972 my wife asked how long we were going to baby sit all these pop idols, claiming that it was pure charity and that it actually cost us money. Lill did not like the music and of course that influenced her. But as a wise man is supposed to listen to a wiser wife we handed the business to our auditor. He later made it rich when Benny Andersson continued his musical career with ABBA.

So we closed our books on Fabulous Four and Hep Stars, as we needed room for more profitable work. It was only months before Benny Andersson broke with Hep Stars and joined by Björn Ulvaeus formed ABBA, winning the Eurovision song festival in Brighton in 1972.

The sixties had been great years for the Ottosons. The offices now occupied the whole top floor at Gamla Brogatan 32 with a staff of fifty-five. We did everything from exhibitions in Sao Paolo to design boxes for Gunnebo nails. I recognized myself as a capitalist now but that was no good at a time when the Swedish people was gliding into the Olof Palme atmosphere that resulted in the regular man in the street, the Svensson, in reality seeing it as something bad to be a company director and private enterprise.

"Of course," they said, "you who can write everything off on your business can drive around in a Mercedes and have a house in Djursholm.

I got so tired of the gossiping and back talking about my Mercedes that I bought a five-year-old Volkswagen. I took it to work. I transferred the Mercedes to the company and parked it in a city garage to be used only for business purposes and to drive to clients outside Stockholm. Still when the tax inspector found it in the books he added 8,000 kronor to my taxable income for, as he called it, the privilege to be able to use it whenever I wanted.

When I added all the taxes that I paid, such as income tax, asset tax, real estate tax and a whopping 25% purchase tax, my tax burden reached 116 percent. As a TV personality I was also watched. After having garaged the Mercedes and arriving at a tuxedo event at the Royal Opera in my old Volkswagen, a gossip columnist wrote "Ottoson is now showing off with driving an old Volkswagen to events."

After that an old friend of mine, Henning Sjöström, a famous attorney and once member of the Swedish athletic team, went out and bought a Rolls Royce, only the second in town. He said that if it came to showing off why not go all the way. The other Rolls in Stockholm was owned by the Svenska Dagbladet columnist KardeMumma and I presumed that the king had a couple tucked away in the royal stable.

My friends did well too. Joel Haskel from school soccer days started TunnelbaneReklam for advertising in subway stations. He spread his domain to soccer stadiums and hockey rinks. When Moscow as site for the world ice Hockey Championship refused rink advertising, Joel almost toppled the event. Moscow had to give. As so many other Swedes of his generation he moved out of the country, to Brussels, keeping just a summerhouse in Sweden.

My social life evolved a lot around friends like him and actors like Gösta Pryzelius who recently passed away after thirty-five years with the Royal Dramatic Theater and several films with Ingemar Bergman. Towards the end of his career he starred in Sweden's most popular TV series, Rederiet (The Shipping Line). He became so popular as the shipper that one of the Stockholm dailies after his death carried the headline "He was not God, but close to it."

How close were my friends, the 22's as we called ourselves? Well, when years later, over in the U.S., I was struggling to run a weekly newspaper and to find capital to expand it I received a surprise visit. Joel Haskel arrived unannounced to my office and put a check for

$30,000 on my desk.

"For your damn paper", he said and waved away an IOU meaning he did not believe that this paper would ever generate enough surplus to pay him back. Of course he was right. I was able to reciprocate only many years later. Of course I get - perhaps unduly - sentimental when I think of the 22s of whom only the glorious opera diva Kjerstin Dellert and I still remain and are as active as ever.

The old ladies are still around. Old wives have a habit to outlive their men. I see Eva, Gösta Pryzelius's wife, when in Sweden. He was born in the house at Polhemsgatan in Stockholm where he died. He was in many of Ingmar Bergman's films. Bergman called him 'Pålitliga Prysse' (Dependable Prysse).

Before he reached the heights from the TV series he did better than most actors. Aside from his salary from the Dramatic Theater, he read Today's Poem over the radio, served as un-announced school radio voice and narrated industrial films and commercials. He was also one of the pillars of the Swedish Actors' Guild. The day before he died he asked to be taken around town to see once more the city he loved dressed in the colors of spring.

He died in his bed with an unfinished letter to me on his lap on May 15, 2000. Gösta loved to, as he said, ta sig ett järn, get a shot of iron (a schnapps of aquavit), or two. I had never been much of a fan of Swedish aquavit so when Gösta came over for a visit of some weeks he left the dinner table once or twice every meal for a couple of minutes. I wondered why. The explanation came when the two of us were flying to New Orleans. At the airport he took his bag to a wastebasket and deposited two empty bottles of aquavit.

When asked why he carried empty liquor bottles around, he said he was embarrassed to have my wife find them. So what are friends for? I got myself a couple of bottles from Swedish friends and took an "iron" or two at every meal to keep him company.

Gösta was a patriarch in a country where family togetherness is getting rare. He had fifty years with his Eva, children and grandchildren and great grandchildren. Did I love that man? You bet.

THE BAHAMAS ADVENTURE

In February of 2002 Swedish television ran an hour-long program called Great Exuma. It was about a young man's journey to an island in the Bahamas to find a piece of land that his grandmother had bought.

On the hills behind the small town of Georgetown on the island of Great Exuma he found the piece of land his grandmother once had been dreaming about during wintry days in Sweden. She had been dreaming about an island house - in which to store her dreams, just as a couple of hundred other Swedes who bought a dream out there. I was the one who had sold them the dream.

One day when I sat in my office in Chicago I saw an ad in the paper about paradise lots in the Bahamas for fifty dollars a month. I thought it seemed a bit suspicious but bought one out of curiosity. Seller was a company called Bahamas Acres Ltd out of Miami. Owner was a Frank Magnuson whose father was from a small town in Småland (I thought that sounded reliable). The father emigrated to the US and pioneered the low installment selling of land in Florida, simply by knocking on doors. He kept the deed of the land sales contract until the plot of land was paid in full.

The Exumas consist of a long chain of small islands

and keys about half an hour by air from Nassau or 45 minutes from Miami. About a thousand people live on Great Exuma. They stem from slaves that the British set ashore on different islands in the Bahamas. Every load of slaves tended to come from the same area in West Africa and most likely from the same tribe. As the British put the slaves ashore in the vast archipelago they also spread local African languages and cultures across the archipelago. Therefore you will find, to this day, distinct differences in folklore between some of the islands. On Great Exuma most of the forefathers came from the Yoruba tribe in western Nigeria while on the next island, Long Island, most have an Ibo heritage from eastern Nigeria. That has proved of importance in the development of the islands. Yoruba are known for business and achievements. Yoruba is the most influential tribe in Nigeria and its work habits and thrift are reflected on Great Exuma. The most famous offspring of Great Exuma are Sidney Poitier and the actress Esther Rolle from Rolltown on the island. One of the leading last names in Bahamas is Rolle.

I flew from Miami to see what I had bought and what Magnuson's development was all about. The land proved to be bushes and cactus with midget palms and crab grass. At Peace and Plenty, Georgetown's combination of a 30 room hotel and restaurant with a famous sailors bar. The town's anchorage, Elizabeth Harbor is the last port for big yachts before tackling the Atlantic. Next stop: Portugal.

From the hills of Exuma you look out over the clearest water in the world. It is as clear as, well, gin. Contributing to this is the fact that there are no streams or rivers in the Bahamas to bring sediments into the ocean. Then there is the Gulf Stream that removes what comes out of the Caribbean and from the rivers of Florida.

It also used to be a peaceful region. When I asked for

a key to my room at the Peace and Plenty, the hotelier said, "We don't have any."

I met Frank Magnuson. In passing he said that "maybe you can sell a lot or two for me in Europe." He gave me the rights to sell his Bahamas Acres properties.

I did not do much about it when I returned home. Then one day Frank sent me $1,000 for advertising to pressure me to do something. I put a coupon ad in the evening papers and within a week I had over thousand coupons back. Neither Frank Magnuson nor I had believed that I would sell more than perhaps a dozen lots. We were apparently on the threshold of something big.

Within the first six months I had sold over five hundred lots on Great Exuma. And earned in the neighborhood of half a million dollars.

Of course I wondered for a while about what I had gotten myself involved in. I told myself that I had to get people out there so they could see for themselves what they had bought. Thus I arranged a tour to Exuma for Christmas 1964.

It was during this trip that the grandmother from the TV program saw her lot. Of the 107 lot owners that came with me no one cancelled. Still the charter trip almost did not happen. We had chartered a Boeing 707 from Pan Am and scheduled a tour for December 20. We would fly via Boston to Miami where we would switch to three DC 3s that could land at the island's much smaller airport.

December 13, the Swedish Civil Aviation Authorities informed us that we did not qualify for a charter across the Atlantic. They would not give us a starting permit. Permits were only given to non-commercial bodies, like Friends of Small Birds etc. "You find a solution. You always do," said my wife.

That's when I came to think of what I learned from the administrator in Lubero in Belgian Kongo: Follow the law to the letter and you find a solution.

Any individual can charter a plane and fly across the Atlantic. He can bring non-paying guests. The size of the plane and the number of guests is irrelevant. The key is, that it's your plane and your guests. So I rapidly returned the trip money and invited all on board as my guests. (With the understanding that they pay upon arrival on Exuma).

The Civil Aviation guys were upset but could not do a thing.

On that plane was the happiest group of Swedes I had ever seen and I just prayed that they would like the island. We landed at Logan International Airport in Boston to refuel. After an hour over the loudspeaker came: Jet Clipper Ottoson departure from Gate 17.

One of the great moments in my life!

We had paid Pan Am $125,000 for the charter and now we were home so to say, and the hysteric activity that had dominated the office lately had finally been laid to rest.

Civil Aviation guys in Stockholm fumed when they discovered that indeed my Exuma guests had not paid a transatlantic penny. But they had paid a stiff sum for a 49-minute return flight Miami-Exuma.

We did not just take over Peace and Plenty but also the Two Turtles Inn and every guestroom we could find in Georgetown.

Several of the Swedes spent hours every day poking around their lots and making future plans together.

This rather loud group shook the lazy latitudes of Great Exuma into action every night. And we gave constable Rolle his first experience of car jacking. A couple of teenagers from the group one night "borrowed" one of the cars on the island for a joy ride to find some action elsewhere. Constable Rolle had a problem. First of all, he did not want to interfere with the group that kept spending so much money on the island. Second problem was that he had no cell to put anyone in. So the moment passed, the constable was given a nice Christmas present and the whole episode was forgotten.

The island justice system was relatively simple, but effective and that's why there were no hotel room keys. The few crimes that were committed on the island resulted in a perpetrator being frozen out of society. No one talked to him, not even the family. Everyone turned the back on him. It was effective enough.

But it was never a crime to drive drunk. DUI did simply not exist. One night I saw the constable help a rather intoxicated guide of ours, Kermit Ferguson, into his car and put the keys in the ignition.

"Are you really going to allow him to drive in that condition?" I said

"How else is he going to get home?" said Rolle "He can't walk".

All together I doubt that there were more than fifty full paying jobs on the island. The rest lived by fishing and catching lobster. There were also a few tomato growers who sent their boxes by the mail boat to Nassau once a week.

The Two Turtles Inn was a sort of driftwood built Inn by a former U.S. Air force fighter pilot, Charlie. I have forgotten his last name. His wife Karin was Swedish. They had run a place in Nassau but moved to Great Exuma when they found it too hectic in the city. Charlie stood behind the bar and anyone who came in with a tie; he cut it off and nailed it to his wall collection. He flew his plane to Nassau for supplies, returning after dark and at least a quart of whiskey. He circled low over town signaling three drivers that he was coming in to land so they'd better get to the airport and shine him in with their headlights. With his Swedish wife he moved to Turks and Caicos a couple of years later when they felt that Exuma got too crowded. They built Three Turtles Inn. Later, while flying in to Turks and Caicos from Nassau on I suppose more than a quart of scotch he came in too low, did not reach the runway and crashed in the sea. They never retrieved his body.

Having done so well for Magnuson I began to play with the idea of starting something on my own in the area. About the same as Bahamas Acres but a bit more upscale. A bank connection put me in contact with Bonniers Publishing House in Sweden and the Maersk Shipping Line in Denmark; we formed a company Elizabeth Harbor Estates Ltd. Simon Bonnier of Sweden's largest publishing house and a young lawyer Utzen Sørensen for the Maersk Line, the world's largest freight and tanker fleet with a refinery on Grand Bahama, joined me in the search of island land. We searched Cat Island, Long Island, Abaco and Harbor Island but kept coming back to Great Exuma. I did not feel too happy about being wall to wall with the Magnusson development. I offered him a cooperative agreement but he declined and wished us luck.

When you deal with commercial giants like Maersk and Bonniers it's hard to get them together for meetings when you deem it needed. Then Bahamas separated from Britain and elected a native government that replaced the old Bay Street Boys. And that did not sit well with my partners.

I replaced them with three entrepreneurs who were easier to work with and each could work actively with construction and infrastructure.

There was Rickard Samuelsson; a builder who they said was responsible for half the city of Vetlanda. He sold us all the tractors and loaders we needed as he wrote them off his books. The second partner was Bernhard Mannberg, a road contractor from Västerås. The third was Folke Olsson of Fribohus, one of Sweden's largest manufacturers of prefabricated wooden houses. It seemed I had an ideal combination of partners.

Elizabeth Harbor Estates Ltd finally bought 1,500 acres of land on Great Exuma bordering Georgetown. When we previously were looking for land, most of the time we were told to see Sir Harold Christie, dean of the Bay Street Boys who had run the colony for years.

The Bay Street Boys all descended from wreck plunderers and rumrunners. Each family had an assigned island where any stranded ship was its prey. To lure ships into dangerous waters these guys lit bonfires on the islands to mislead shippers. The Bahamas waters were hard to navigate. These plundering rights were entered into Bahama's constitution and were actually in force all the time to the Second World War.

Wreck plunderers like Sir Harold Christie and Sir Stafford Sands switched to rum running during the Prohibition in the U.S. They made a lot of money and with that bought themselves influence and respect.

When Edward abdicated his British throne so he could marry Mrs. Simpson, the Crown made him governor of the Bahamas, one of the smallest and most insignificant British colonies. I am sure the British government was happy with the Simpson affair to get Edward off the throne. He had great assets and businesses in Germany at the beginning of WWII. A British King with German assets did not sit very well.

In the Bahamas the Duke and Duchess of Windsor were soon joined by one of the wealthiest men in the world, the Swede Axel Wenner-Gren, founder of Electrolux. He tied his mega yacht, the world's largest, which once belonged to Barbara Hutton, at Hog Island, today Paradise Island. Wenner-Gren wanted to come to the U.S. but the Americans saw him as too German friendly. Marguerite Wenner-Gren who wore jewelry up to her elbows and the duchess got along fabulously. So did

Wenner-Gren and the Duke. Wenner-Gren had access to banks and money in Germany. Regularly he sent his Swedish "runner" Andersson to Germany to pick up cash and fly with it to banks in Mexico. He got millions of the duke's assets out of Germany.

One day a funny little man arrived to Nassau. He and his old dog had spent a dozen years in Klondike looking for gold. One day he struck the mother load and instantly became the richest man in the world. He did not like the taxes in Canada so he moved to the Bahamas where, of course, all the financial vultures descended on him. He was Harry Oakes.

During an elaborate dinner on Wenner-Gren's yacht, a female guest of Mrs. Simpson pointed at Harry Oakes and asked who he was. "Oh," said the Duchess, "he is the Charlie Chaplin of the islands."

When Sir Harry Oakes - yes he had been honored by the Crown - felt that the Bay Street Boys had taken him for enough money - including building Harry Oakes International Airport, he was found murdered in his home one morning. A gardener had seen a speedboat come and go with some men spending half an hour in the house.

At the same time, the gardener saw Sir Harold Christie's Rolls Royce drive the speed boaters from Miami to and from the house. Sir Harry's son in law was accused of the murder that overshadowed the war headlines on the front pages of the world's newspapers. At the trial you saw as reporters both Ernest Hemingway and Erle Stanley Gardner. The gardener was never found and the chief of police who believed in the young man's innocence was transferred out of the country. Finally the son in law was freed on condition that he leave the Bahamas.

Axel Wenner-Gren tried for many years to be allowed to build a bridge from his Hog Island to the city of Nassau. When denied he sold the island and purchased land on Andros Island. Hog Island was renamed Paradise Island. Marguerite Wenner-Gren's painting studio by the dockside is now the popular Restaurant Marguerite. The Bahamians liked Harry Oakes and Axel Wenner-Gren, but could just as well have been without the Duke and his wife.

The murder of Sir Harry Oakes and stories about Axel Wenner-Gren were still fresh when I first visited the Bahamas. I remember that during my first taxi ride from the airport to Harold Christie's office on Bay Street, the driver pointed at the sign and said: "So you are going to see the guy that had Harry Oakes murdered."

Harold Christie had his finger in almost every land deal in the Bahamas. He did not own big acreage but had secured small important parcels of land and of course he was an agent for most. On every island that Simon Bonnier and I visited for land purposes we found a couple of acres here and a couple of acres there belonging to Christie. It was for instance where you had to put a bridgehead or anchor a dock. Clever old bastard.

Although both Maersk and Bonniers backed out of the project after a year, I am grateful for the experience to discuss and plan the Flamingo Bay project with them. Maersk, a Russian from St. Petersburg came to Denmark with a coastal runner and built the world's largest tanker fleet. His philosophy was that if he had to dock a ship he would only have to pay for a night watch man. Once when Onassis was in trouble and asked Maersk for a loan he answered that he did not lend money for ships sailing under convenience flag.

Almost every day I see Maersk containers everywhere on the roads and stacked in the hundreds at the Port of Miami. Headquarter for this mega undertaking was at the City Hall Square ('Rådhuspladsen') in Copenhagen. All that marked the importance of the building was (and perhaps still is) a one square foot brass plate by the entrance

I can't withhold you this story. Maersk having gas and oil concessions in the North Sea was asked by the government to contribute to a housing project for the oil rig workers' families. He refused until the Danish finance minister flustered asked him why.

"Because," said Maersk and slammed his big fist on the table, "it is my money and I don't want to."

I guess you cannot get a clearer answer than that.

When Maersk and Bonnier after a year of preparations sold out to my new less internationally experienced partners, I should perhaps have taken heed. The early partners simply did not trust investing in colored countries heading for self-rule.

With my new partners I aimed at the U.S. market with offices in Nassau and Miami. But first we had to get permits to sell real estate on contracts. The laws were different in every state. Florida Land Sales Board was the toughest to get a permit from. The application contained 180 pages. Most states asked for the same information about the project, and us but there was always something that differed from state to state to slow us down.

Consulting an attorney in Miami about how much he would charge to complete our Florida application. About $20,000 he said. Can you imagine what that would be in today's money!

I pondered how it could be done cheaper and found that the cheapest would of course be if I made it myself. I figured looking at all the forms that an attorney could not answer most of the questions and provide all the information unless he asked me.

So I did it. Over 200 pages. With it all I went to the Land Sales Board in Tampa.

I presented the documents to a development director, a rather tough official known for sending many directors home for more info, I put on a bit of extra accent when I explained that due to my limited knowledge of English I might have misunderstood some of the questions.

"Let's see", he said and read through the whole application and made corrections.

"This will do it," he said

When we finally had it developed, with the help of a Swedish architect in Stockholm, I took the master plan for the about 1,500 acres to the same inspector who had helped me in Tampa. From there I handed it to The Ministry of Works in Nassau. Next I got us an attorney, Nigel Bowe, a young man just recently graduated. We took him from his job at Dupuch and Turnquest in Nassau and helped him into his own office. We needed him amongst other things for deed processing.

One of the first tasks in the Bahamas was to invite the Minister of Works, Livingstone Coakley, to the island. We had tried to see him several times before but he had always been out fishing. Well here was indeed an opportunity to go fishing.

We started with fine road making equipment, loaders, dump trucks and a Swedish machine operator. But he, like the Swedish guy after him, did not last long. They did not last. Long periods of loneliness led to drinking sprees at Two Turtles and Peace and Plenty. The first operator's wife left for home after a month and the second wife after six weeks. The lack of hair salons took its toll. The men began sitting at the bars a bit too much and I had to send them home. I finally found an American engineer who had worked on projects in the desert and loneliness of Arizona and Nevada. All he demanded was beer in the refrigerator and a long weekend in Miami every month.

Our clubhouse on a hill overlooking a small beach proved an ideal home with a second floor apartment for the sales manager Richard Tanner and his wife. They had fled the hustle in Connecticut by selling their auto dealership, bought a yacht, headed for Bahamas and landed at my dock in Flamingo Bay. As Tanner said, "you just can't fish all day."

Celebrities and other prominent guests started to show at the clubhouse. The first was the prominent ocean sailor, Captain Fuller of Fuller Brush Company. He built himself a house with a wide view over the ocean. Then for $20,000 he added a small building to house his model trains.

Robert Mitchum docked in Elizabeth Harbor one day. We shared some beer in the clubhouse and he bought a lot. He told me to pick a top lot and send the contract to his yacht that by the way, was surrounded by small vessels with women wanting a glimpse of the star.

Does anyone of you remember from the Beatles era the song "I beg your pardon; I never promised you a rose garden?" I can't remember the name of the girl who made it popular but she spent a couple of weeks with us at the island and bought two lots... (Ed. note: It could have been British Sandie Shaw or American Lynn Anderson)

Doing so well in the Bahamas and my frequent presence there created a small problem at home. I could not tell my PR and advertising customers that I could not see them for instance on a Friday and Monday because I was going to the Bahamas. But they would accept that I took a long weekend to fix my summerhouse, just like they did. I left Thursday afternoons and was back in the office Tuesday morning.

The pressure was intense, but inspiring. The land business boomed and Folke Olsson of Fribohus built a plant for trusses and wall elements on the island.

It was great years for the Bahamas. Freeport on Grand Bahama grew with high-rise condos and there were projects all over Eleuthera, Abaco, Long Island and Bimini and of course around the capitol of Nassau. The Lyford Key on New Providenc became like a Bahamian Hampton.

Nigel Bowe grew fatter and fatter and his wristwatches went from Rolex to Patek Philippe. But apparently not thanks to our legal paper work. He had native friends in high places.

And somewhere in the background worked his pal, the PLP (Peoples Liberal Party) chairman Lyndon Pindling on the people's revolution. It's amazing that the Bay Street Boys and their republican party did not understand what was on its way, not even when they got their majority in the Parliament cut to three and shortly thereafter in a new election lost the majority to the PLP.

Still, no one believed that a government under Pindling would totally bankrupt the country. All foreigners' work permits were immediately revoked and the unemployment reached 70 percent. A Greek family that had run a restaurant for 30 years was given two weeks to get out. The big 400-room Royal Caribbean Hotel had only a night manager with a permit while management was given to a man who was the bartender and trade union leader. Suddenly we had no engineer, surveyor, heavy equipment operator and no manager. And there was no one at the bank on the island. I had to have a man on the island. What was it I said before about following the law to the letter? Foreigners were still allowed to tend to their homes and gardens etc. It never said anything about restrictions to the size of the garden. Mine was 1,500 acres. I sent my son Lars to watch over it saving what could be saved.

The Bahamas deteriorated. No one took care of the infrastructure; squatters filled up the condos in Freeport and just settled in empty vacation cottages. The idea from the government was to force foreign entrepreneurs to hire Bahamian staff. But there was none. I could not even get a person to run a front loader.

Almost every foreigner who had a job in the Bahamas for banks, insurance brokers, airlines, builders, hotels, shops etc. were shown the door. It was said that the power behind the immigration minister Hanna was his wife. She was a pub owner's daughter from Wales. She had met and married Hanna when he studied in Cardiff. The British had all rejected her for marrying a black man and now she was paying them back. It was said that Mrs. Hanna had provided her husband with names of all the white people he ought to deport.

Couldn't we have foreseen this said Folke Olsson's son Gösta in 2002. Looking back into the development of so many colonies wouldn't it have flagged warnings early on?

It may seem so. But Bahamas was by most regarded as different. The Royal Bank of Canada and Barclays of London both told us that the Bahamas was like the Rock of Gibraltar. That is until they sat there stripped of staff themselves. Nassau had almost spilled over with foreign banks and Pan Am had started regular flights to Eleuthera. We had a so-called revolving credit with Chase Manhattan Bank in Nassau, which was to be substituted by a long-term mortgage. Instead the bank called the $1,4 million for payment within two weeks.

The demand came from New York because of the bank's problems in Nassau. As a result I went to Sir Harold Christie who was a Chase Manhattan board member. We still owed him some money. He assured me not to worry. He was going to straighten out the bank as soon as he came back from a European trip the following week.

He never came back. He died in his hotel room in London.

Sir Harold had a brother that he had used more or less as an errand boy over the years, He took the $300,000 note still remaining on the $2 million purchase and sold it to a crooked speculator, Frank Hart, on Paradise Island who blew the bank on the mortgage. Behind the scenes our trusted attorney Nigel Bowe, who had visited us so many times in Sweden, played for his own gain behind our backs.

It might not have had to go the way it finally did had it not been for my partners' insistence to keep everything in writing in Sweden instead of being satisfied with keeping the books in Nassau or Miami. At the time Sweden had currency restrictions. You could only export a limited amount for personal use or to meet Swedish business obligations.

One day the Swedish IRS came to Fribohus for a surprise tax control visit. There on the shelf was a file titled Bahamas. It told how Olsson had traveled to Hamburg to send thousands to the Bahamas and likewise Mannberg and Samuelsson. The IRS in Sweden grabbed their passports, closed their bank accounts. They came to my office, found nothing improper. The money I had made as an agent for Magnusson I had kept and paid taxes on in the United States.

What Fribohus failed to explain was that they were seeking an export market in the Bahamas and had already a truss and wall factory on the island. I presumed that when they saw the headlines of their "misdeeds" they panicked.

I tried to save what could be saved. However, his brother and Frank Hart and Nigel Bowe, now carted off all the books that I had taken to Sir Harold's office on Bay Street while transferring my office to his. They blew the bank and us. I felt it was unfathomable that a smart man like Richard Samuelsson had not applied a long time ago for fund transfers to establish an export market on the Bahamas. I remember the tabloids' headlines:

The company director's secret book reveals the tax fraud.

All the prosecutor had to do was to sit down and read it.

The only consolation was that the roof caved in on the hotel Nigel Bowe had just built on Great Exuna. We had helped this man to a career. We trusted him.

Nigel Bowe played his political cards well - too well I would say. He became a trusted advisor to Premier Lyndon Pindling. And he made big money for himself and the prime minister in the drug market.

The Drug Enforcement Agency in United States had kept an eye for a long time on the Bahamas as a transfer post for drugs to the U.S. The smugglers that kept paying their dues to Pindling et consortes had no problems. They could even land on the airfield we built on Great Exuma, refuel at a price and continue to some private airport in the United States,

Those that did not pay attention to the Bahamian government's cash requirements were arrested and put in the Fox Hill prison in Nassau. Nigel Bow was then appointed defense attorney to a fee of $200,000, which it is said he split with Pindling. There is no good reason to doubt that.

DEA had for some time had its eyes on Nigel Bowe attributed to the knowledge of bags of cash from members of a Colombian drug cartel members distributed to officials in the Bahamas. In 1985 a grand jury in Miami accused Nigel Bowe of overseeing transportation via the Bahamas to USA of more than a ton of cocaine and of taking big sums of money to protect narcotic smugglers from the police in the Bahamas.

Shortly thereafter, in 1995, it was revealed how Bowe used airports on the outer islands and mostly the Flamingo Bay airport that we built, to service planes transporting narcotics from Colombia. The U.S. press described Nigel Bowe as a close friend of Prime Minister Pindling and a flamboyant Nassau attorney wearing a lot of gold and living in a stately mansion and as a man who loves nights out on town.

The U.S. Attorney's Office tried for several years to get Nigel Bowe handed over to the American authorities in compliance with the agreement that existed between the countries. However, the authorities in the Bahamas were not too anxious to deport one of the prime minister's best friends. It took almost ten years before he appeared in front of an American judge. In February of 1994 he was sentenced to 15 years in prison.

"Allow me to say most humbly," Bowe said with choking voice when appearing in front of district judge Lawrence King, "that I swear that I am innocent. I am here only because of the pressure by the United States on the small country of the Bahamas to deport me."

Simultaneously with Bowe's trial there were charges against Orville "Tiny" Turnquest, deputy prime minister and the country's second man with charges that he had worked for one of the biggest narcotics kings of all time, the head of the Medellin cartel Carlos Lehder Rivas who owned an island in the Exuma Chain and had Bowe as his lawyer.

Like rings on water the corruption spread through government offices and ministries.

Among Pindling's closest friends was Everett Bannister who stayed on the outside to be able to work better as an entrepreneur. He knew the U.S. from years as a doorman at a nightclub in New York. Then there was the agricultural minister (which included fishery) George A Smith. He drove around in Nassau in a BMW that he received from Lehder. On Exuma he had his eye on a strip of land, like a small peninsula, on which our latest engineer had built five beach type cottages.

He asked for the price and got the reply $250,000.

"You mean $25,000," said Smith.

"No, $250,000 and not a penny less".

"We'll see about that," added Smith

Our engineer, who had stayed behind on the island and was engaged to a local girl, was told that his visa had expired. He left and came back a month later with a week's permit to stay. He found the road to his property blocked by big boulders. The police explained that the road was closed for traffic, as it did not comply with the 22 feet width to allow traffic. That road had been marked on maps since 1890. But it was just 20 feet. The owner sent in applications of exemption from widening or to allow restricted traffic. They all came back non-read and without comments. Smith got the land after a year's harassment. The moment he took over the property, the road boulders disappeared and the road was put back into traffic.

Harold Christie's brother had only one interest - to get as much cash as fast as possible. He sold our $300,000 note to Harold Christie for $400,000 to Frank Hart, a crook who lived in a $4,000 a month house on Paradise Island, hiding from the police of both Canada and USA. For the four hundred thousand he got over a million dollars worth of land contracts from customers in USA and Canada, which generated enough cash to keep the project in moth balls for the time being.

Maybe it was just as well that we were hit the first robber year of the Pindling administration. But it is said that sometimes in the years ahead even the devil starts to believe in God. So when the big casino companies began investing in the Bahamas as a gamblers' paradise, a bunch of ministers suddenly tried to revert from the image of robber barons to, if not exactly respected, at least accepted politicos. Whatever and however, that year is one that none of us will ever forget. I think Rickard Samuelsson, who was said to have built half the city of Vetlanda, never before felt such stimulation in life.
So far his emotional highs had been to buy a new Mercedes every year. I never forget that day at Christmas

1970 when the two of us dined at the MS Queen Elizabeth when anchored in the Port of Ft. Lauderdale. I got him to share a bottle of wine.

After a couple of glasses he turned around and nipped the butt of the girl who served us. The adventure of his year in the Bahamas must have been a high of life for the steadfast and likeable Samuelsson.

I felt safe in many ways with these both hard working, and knowledgeable entrepreneurs. Bernhard Mannberg steady, Folke Olsson always calculating. The four of us were so much more than partners. We were friends. They are all gone now. I was the one who got them into this and they should have had many reasons to blame me for the misfortune. But there was not a word of criticism from anyone of them.

Footnote—Miami Herald, September 18, 1985:
F. Nigel Bowe, the most prominent criminal lawyer in the Bahamas was charged Wednesday with supervising the transportation of thousands of pounds of cocaine from Columbia through the islands into the United States. A twenty-count indictment also says that Bowe shielded cocaine dealers from the Bahamian police in exchange for large sums of cash and met with smugglers in outlaying Bahamian islands to find landing strips for drug planes making the long flight from Colombia. "If we can take a person like him out of the operation, it makes a dramatic impact on drug smuggling in the United States" said Robert Dempsey, US Law Enforcement Commissioner.

Towards the end of 1972 when we all felt that the Nassau political structure was breaking apart, I moved the company office to Miami and hoping to possibly find a buyer of the project. It was of course a very distant hope as the reputation of the Bahamas was badly damaged. I had put my share in Elizabeth Harbor Estate Ltd. in cash, from income earned during my time with Frank Magnuson. I never got involved with the Swedish tax authorities the way my partners did.

We all had signed personally for the Chase Manhattan loan and the bank soon attacked my partners in Sweden. At the time there were still export restrictions for Swedish currency, which also had been the basis for the accusation from the Swedish authorities against my partners. However, Chase thought of what they believed would be a smart way to get the money by making a Swedish bank claim it. Svenska Handelsbanken, I think it was, claimed the money and spent thousands on lawyers. The judge did not buy it. He simply stated the currency export ban on an eventually illegal money affair realizing that once Handelsbanken was paid, a transfer would be made to Chase.

But then Chase remembered that they had Ottoson living in the United States and decided to go after me for the whole sum. I had no money and no intention to pay. They took a risk in the Bahamas and were hammered there losing their staff just as we. Why should they get away with it? Called to a deposition they looked sternly at me and asked me to list my assets. I told them I had rent and food money and a bicycle worth about $50 that they could have.

"Mr. Ottoson, this is no joke."

"I fully realize that, but if you think I will pay $1.4 million dollars to you for a defunct Bahamian corporation, you must be kidding. Why don't you ask the new landowner for the money? He blew you, didn't he?"

That I stayed in America after the Bahamian collapse was due to a marital conflict after 33 years. My wife felt that the house in Djursholm was too big for us now when the children were gone. She wanted an apartment in the city. I believe something could have been worked out but she took it upon herself to make the sale of my dream house and told me in the car after she picked me up at Arlanda airport:

"By the way, darling, I sold the house."

She had already bought a two-bedroom apartment. I refused to move in. I stayed in the house until the furniture was gone and then took a plane back to Miami.

LARS-HENRIK OTTOSON

AMERICA HERE I COME

From being somebody in Sweden I became nobody in America. Fortunately it was a bit easier to get a green card in the 1970's and less costly than it is today. Still it took over two years and $50,000 in a business with at least one U.S. employee.

I spent time in Sweden and in the Bahamas as I went in and out of the US when my tourist visas expired.

Don't kid yourself that you can put anything over on the U.S. immigration. I tried once to just spend a couple of weeks in the Bahamas and then get in on a new tourist visa. The U.S. Immigration officer, stationed in the Bahamas, asked me where I resided. I told him Sweden.

"It seems to me you spend more time living in the US," he said and ordered me to be at the immigration office in Miami in two weeks. And he took my passport.

Was this the end of my American dream? Should my green card application now be cancelled? The two weeks were the longest in my life, all the while thrown between hopes and doubts. Then came the day when I sat there in the waiting room filled with fear. I must have urinated a dozen times as my nerves upset my body functions. The room was packed with Cubans and Haitians and other stray types. One by one they were

The entrance to TrailInn.

entering the cubicle of some immigration officer. After a few minutes he called a guard saying: "Take this man down to interrogation."

After hearing that repeated for several hours, I was not very optimistic. I actually believed that I was looking at my last days in America. The officer looked through my passport and asked how many days I had stayed in America the previous year. "At least 270," I said. No use lying to a well informed immigration officer.

"Almost right, 276 as a matter of fact. And the previous year?"

"Almost the same."

"You can say that again. You know you are only allowed to stay six months any given year. So do you think I should deport you or send you to the stockade? However, I see here that you have done a lot of valuable work for the US Department of Commerce back ten years ago, you had a company in Chicago and have been employed by Ford Motor so I think I'll let you have another three months here to put your house in order. Welcome again to the U.S., Mr. Ottoson."

He had every date on me since 1950.

Fortunately I was well prepared for my green card. I had the requested $50,000 invested in a U.S. company, SASOCO, and a U.S. employee. We had the agency for a German cosmetic company, Sans Soucis from Baden Baden. It was not my line of business but it had to do because it suited my American fiancé Karin who was German and familiar with the product.

To land in the INS special file is not very good. Simon Bonnier learned that. For some time he headed a department store that Bonniers owned on Manhattan. When the Vietnam War erupted and the military started looking in their books for eligible young men for the army, Simon moved back to Sweden. It did apparently not sit well with the authorities in America. For years later every time Simon arrived in America, if only to change planes at Kennedy Airport to continue to the Bahamas, the passport police hauled him in for hour-long questionings because his name was in the Big Book. He had papers from the U.S. Embassy in Stockholm and from the Department of Commerce. When we arrived together, we always agreed ahead of the passport inspection in which airport restaurant I should wait for him. I have filled a lot of cross word puzzles at airport restaurants.

I met Karin at actor/director Alf Kjellin's home on Mulholland Drive in Beverly Hills. She was one of the health guru Jack la Lane's best assistants and at 40 could still do a flip flop like a 17 year old. She was a flexibility trainer for many stars and had a health food store in Ventura. She was born Karin Nonnast in Leipzig in Germany and married a U.S. airplane inspector. He moved from airport to airport, from motel to motel. She wanted a home. Well, she got me.

It was hard for a Swede who was used to wear the pants in the family to adjust to the more spouse equal condition in an American marriage. Swedish women were strong and efficient but generally let the men make the big family decisions. It took three visits from Karin before I dared to let her stay. I suppose she was also a bit doubtful about me.

In the beginning I did most things wrong. Such as buying her a car. Unfortunately the wrong car; a small one.

"What's that," said Karin. Here I thought that I had been generous. Most men in Europe don't buy cars for their wives.

"I'll send for my car from Ventura," she said. One day arrived a Jaguar, not the latest model but still a Jaguar. Sans Soucis featured the world's first full natural line of cosmetics from own farms and waters. Karin went on a sales tour to drug stores and salons around Florida. I served as delivery boy and shelf checker for some time until I could find some more stimulating work on my own. I learned a lot about the fight for shelf inches in the stores and how to reward (entice) the counter girls with gratifications for recommending your product. I learned such totally useless things as that the women of Miami Beach liked bright red nail polish, the Cuban women liked it darker while on the west coast pink was the big seller. I learned that in Miami bills took 60 to 90 days to get paid while up in Vero Beach and over in St Petersburg they were paid within 30 days. If you are familiar with Florida's population structure you know why.

I had now spent almost all of the requested fifty thousand on an American business and I estimated it would take some time for Sasoco to return any profit. We were up there against some heavy market hitters and the German company had no feeling for give-aways - such as buy one, get one free etc. The Germans would not support that kind of waste.

Pondering all this I sat one night at the bar of the English pub on Key Biscayne - a place made famous as president Nixon's favorite place when dining with banker pal Bebe Reboso. Next to me sat a guy who obviously had a problem because he looked miserable. He told me that he had retired from the Air Force with the rank of colonel and had bought a couple of free weeklies, which were now running away with his money. When he told me that he had a staff of nine I asked him what they were all doing. Three did ad hunting and the rest made the paper. I said he should keep the ad girls, fire the rest and hire an editor and a typesetter.

"Is that so, and how do you know," the colonel asked. I explained that I used to edit a 40 page daily paper. I sort of tried to tell him that his weekly I could do left-handed. If there was anything I could do it was a newspaper.
So the colonel said that if I was so sure I could do it for him, then I could start Tuesday after he fired the present editor.

Tuesday arrived. I had started my lunch when the colonel rang and wondered where the hell I was. I told him that I believed we had had too much to drink and that it was all drunk bar talk.

"I am never too drunk not to remember making an agreement."

That's why we moved from Key Biscayne to Pompano Beach and a place in Lighthouse Point. I took over Herald Publishing Company that issued the Pompano Beach local Weekly Herald and a mobile home park paper for southern Florida and a special newspaper for the Indian (Native American) Seminole tribe called Alligator Times with the subheading "The Independent Newspaper of the Sovereign Nation of the Seminole Tribe." I was suddenly the only non-Indian editor of a Native American newspaper in the U.S. Of course it had a figurehead editor-in-chief, Moses Jumper.

Pompano Beach begins where Fort Lauderdale ends. It had at the time a population of about 80,000, and was best known as winter home for quarter horse racing and home base for the Goodyear Blimp.

We found a house in Lighthouse Point almost next door to Ingemar Johansson and a couple of Swedish trotting horse owners who winter quartered their horses in Pompano and ran at the city's famous race track.

One day an older gentleman with a heavy Swedish accent walked through the doors and said he wanted to place an ad for his wife who was running for mayor. I asked him if he still spoke Swedish. 'Klart som fan' (Sure as hell) he said. The event was in itself not very remarkable until I found that Gunnar Westin had been head of Ford's marine engine division in Stockholm. He had just left the company when I came to Ford and took over his secretary - the one I later met in Cape Town. Mrs. Westin won the election and became mayor. Shortly thereafter she had a stroke and Pompano went again to elect a mayor. The first one who appeared at the paper to place an ad for his wife for mayor had - yes you are right - a heavy Swedish accent. He was horse trainer Carl Olson from Markaryd. Emma Lou Olson, won. As mayor she married my son Lars to his Rita when they came to visit me to tell me the good news.

Incidents like these have followed me through life.

I closed down the mobile home paper. Its unsavory distribution area of mobile home parks spread over half of Florida made it too expensive to distribute. Alligator Times was a great joy to edit. It was the printed voice of Indians in southeast USA and as such was regularly supplied with news from the Bureau of Indian Affairs in Washington. For me as an old news hand it felt very special to edit this paper with the help of its editor Moses Jumper who came to me with his notes and short articles and poems. He was the Brighton Reservation's poet in residence, so to say. Remarkable, wasn't it, that a Swedish journalist comes to America to edit an Indian newspaper, in fact at the time the only Indian newspaper in America.

I had a bit of a problem with how to present my first Christmas issue. I had put together what I thought was a pretty fine front page. Moses just shook his had over both cribs and Santas. That was the first time I had seen him upset and hurt. That he had a biblical first name meant nothing as he gave me a poem to illustrate for the front page. It was called Ode to the Great Spirit.

Weekly Herald was doing all right. I was even able to make the colonel some money. He was actually very satisfied having recouped most of his money. Thus just before Christmas 1978 he announced that he was giving up the paper.

"Make me an offer," he said to which I replied that I had nothing to offer.

"I know that," he answered, " but I will let you have the paper for no set sum, just half of the net you make the next three years".

It was not exactly a Christmas present, more an offer I could not afford to refuse.

I soon understood why he was offering me the paper for half the net profit, if there was a net. He liked me and where he was heading, he did not need any money. That is how his widow explained it.

The first year with me as owner did not start very well.

The typographers went on strike in America. The industry was in that era between lead setting and computers. A whole generation of lead setters was fighting for their jobs, which they inevitably lost in the end. We had a big clumsy Compugraphic Compuwriter that produced text in single columns, which we then pasted on boards with headlines stamped out in various sizes from a headliner. I stood there without both typesetter and board paster. Damn it Lars, you've done this type of work before I told myself - and sat down at the Compuwriter and started to type out columns foot by foot and punching out headlines. I asked advertisers to supply print ready originals. I was typesetting over the weekend and pasting Monday through Tuesday. On Wednesday I finished it in the afternoon, took the boards to Miami where I had found a printer not affected by the strike. I slept on a couch in the printer's office while he produced the paper during the night and I was back up in Pompano at eight in the morning for the distributors to head out. I had chosen Thursday as publishing day to enable me to catch City Hall's weekly sessions and to get as much as I could get from the weekend work of the police for the paper's most popular column: The Police Blotter. The Weekly Herald was the paper to read in Pompano Beach as people looked through the police reports to see if they could find anyone they knew cited.

The years in Pompano Beach were a learning experience when, as a national reporter I now found myself reduced (by myself) to a local reporter of grass roots politics. It gave me a better grip than ever on how the strings run, from local politics up to Tallahassee and from Tallahassee to Washington. As a Swede you learn how much closer and clearer the political picture is on the local level in America than in Sweden, or Denmark, and Norway for that matter. In Sweden you can listen to a town council meeting but you can't open your mouth.

You have your choice every four years to elect your representative. When I took a city council member from Gothenburg to a town hall meeting in Pompano he was almost speechless

"This would never work in Sweden."

"Why not?"

"We are not democratic enough to handle that. It would only end in a shouting match."

I don't know how it happened but one day Karin came home with some scientology ideas that she had picked up while meeting Sasoco customers. Yes, she was still trying to sell the cosmetic line.

I suppose that there are few marriages that don't at some time hit a rock. Karin, who was a very physical person spent evenings when I worked at an exercise studio, teaching and participating. I noticed that she joined some rather expensive courses, just saying she had to improve herself. Then she became sort of absent and then started avoiding me. She had through "friends" been smitten, seduced and defrauded by the church of Scientology. When I asked what these big sums of money bought her she told me that it was none of my business. Her scientology friends labeled me a "covert hostile" and told her to either convert me or divorce me. I slept on the sofa and soon gave up trying to tell her that scientology was a business venture preying on people's needs for a mental crutch and at best a quasi philosophy. Scientology leaders were not welcome in England and the movement was prohibited to operate and recruit in Germany.

I told myself that Karin is intelligent and must, sooner or later, find out for herself. She was told that she should divorce me and that they would easily find her a suitable husband. I knew enough scientology to know that money was the key and once you could not pay for constant improvement courses, to elevate you to new member status, they lost interest in you. They were especially anxious to keep Karin because of her looks. They talked with the headquarters in Clearwater in Florida about using her as a poster girl.

To this day I don't know how I was able to mentally survive those months. But I just refused to be defeated into a divorce ordered by a third party. I constantly reminded myself that Karin's common sense one day would win the battle for me. And so it happened one day! She came to me crying and asked for forgiveness. I had given her that a long time ago. She now at last said she had been captured by lies and deceit.

I had always regarded Scientology as a gimmick created by the old man Hubbard - sort of borderline religion and an out of space alienism with 'better beings' keeping an eye from their space craft on the world of Jesus and Moses. I noticed soon that they never bothered to try to convert any Muslims. I wonder why.

Scientology serves as evidence that there is a market for quasi-religious movements telling you the most obvious things in the most complicated fashion. People, who don't have much self-confidence or believe in their soul, provide easy prey for cults and TV evangelists.

"Pray for me pastor, here is ten bucks." But you better not believe that you can find help and salvation through a movement like Scientology. People like you and I just can't afford it. Scientology is great for John Travolta or Tom Cruise, actors whose lives often are influenced by the roles they play. My acting parents found themselves in Christian Science, B.H (Before Hubbard). They needed a crutch. I remember how my father's mood often changed with the character he played on stage.

To work twelve hours a day, seven days a week with Weekly Herald and Alligator Times and fight for bed and seat with your wife during the rest of the time made a change of job and home seem an attractive alternative for both of us now when Karin had been able to run away from her mental occupiers.

So far life had endowed me with an unusual portion of luck when the going got tough. Once again, Miss Luck smiled at me. Right then a friend called and asked if I might be interested in a marketing job that required knowledge of German and French. If!

We had no problem to move. The house was a rental with an option to buy and we were not buying. It felt a bit sad to leave Ingemar Johansson and friends who had supported me when I needed them. I left the publishing company to the staff on the same conditions as I got it, knowing that one of the guys I had picked as an editorial assistant would be able to take my place.

Thus we returned to Key Biscayne, "Paradise Found" as the bumper stickers bragged.

Honestly, I don't know who had the biggest luck - Roland International that hired me or I. From the years in the Bahamas I knew international real estate better than most and I had contacts all over Europe for the kind of properties Roland intended to market.

The company name came from two partners, Roberts and Friedland who worked side by side in the same office at a super sized desk, like an illustration of good cooperation.

Roland carried some heavy baggage from many years of selling acre lots, site unseen, on contracts in future developments. They sold to people up north who were dreaming of a sunny retirement in Florida. Roland had bought the land for perhaps a couple of hundred an acre and resold it for three or four times that much, building roads and staking out lots. They started the same way as General Development that laid the foundation for Port St. Lucie in Florida, one of the fastest growing cities in the U.S. today. The land that Roland wanted to sell was at the southern tip of Miami, down by the

Homestead Air Force Base. They offered quarter acre lots for between two- and three thousand on contract, much like a contract to buy a car. It was at the zenith of the Florida land boom - almost like a throw back to the twenties when Miami Beach and Coral Gables hit the market - boomed and, by the way, busted, and came back again, stronger than ever. It seems you never know with land. Or, you know but never really learn.

General Development was the world's largest real estate operator, but Roland was not far behind. The main difference was that Roland had a more mixed market product. It included office buildings, hotels, marinas etc. Roland was partner in the famous Fontainebleau Hilton on Miami Beach. They built the luxurious Grand Bay Hotel in Coconut Grove together with Continental Company etc. Question: could I handle both lots and buildings? Of course I could, and they believed I could. The two Rolands were smart. To market hotels, office buildings etc requires capital. Lot sales on contracts create a steady monthly cash flow. The lots brought Roland, I estimated, about a million a month. The Homestead land was added to that part of the finances and the lowest and even the sump land lots were a safe buy located on land that the city of Homestead sooner or later had to annex for expansion.

My first visual contact with General Development was passing their motel size office building on US 1 in the corner of Port St. Lucie Blvd, then just a half a mile long into the bush. GD flew in Europeans bi-weekly, mainly from Germany and sold them first a lot and then a home to put on it. It worked great until someone found out that General Development's overcharges were criminally large, if you can put it that way. Three top GD guys landed in prison for fraud. The corner building where GD had its office is still there I think. Now two six-lane highways meet there. You have come a long way Sancta

Lucia from Sicilian sainthood to name this place of rush and go, one of the five fastest growing cities in the USA. Roland trudged carefully. They never encouraged lot buyers to build. Their line was: Buy it, keep it and make some money on it in the future. At the time European newspapers started to write about the Florida land boom and warned people about buying the swampland. Now the truth is that in south Florida wherever you build, you build on old swampland. From Palm Beach down, there never was much else except a strip a mile wide behind the beach. Palm Beach and Fort Lauderdale would have been half the size today if they had not drained the swamps.

Roland expected me to spend at least half my time in Europe. Roland had an office on Gothestrasse in Frankfurt where Werner Rayman had built up a small but smart operation to sell a thousand or so quarter acre lots in Homestead.

He was apparently not too happy about my arrival on the scene. I think he saw me more as a spy from the head office. In a way maybe you could see it like that because I toured Germany to visit lot owners checking with them about what had been said and promised. I traveled from Hamburg in the north to Freiburg in the south. From Saarbrücken and Frankfurt in the west to Munich in the east. People started to believe me when I said "You should see that dump from the air. Real Swamp. But the location is superb."

The managing director, Bruce Kaye, obviously felt that I would be better suited for some larger and more solid projects than lot sales. For the next seven years I traveled Europe with a portfolio of hi rise office buildings, hotels and condominiums, ski lodges in Colorado and shopping centers here and there. During all these years I was flying between Miami and Frankfurt every month with properties put together especially for pension funds of companies like Unilever, KLM, BP etc. Roland had just moved into newly built office premises in Coconut Grove and together with Continental Companies built Grand Bay Hotel.

Roland helped me to buy a three-story town house on Key Biscayne and Karin went about furnishing it. She had not felt well lately, complaining of almost constant pains in her abdomen. She found it hard to work and gave up her cosmetics business. Biopsies did not show anything until a year later when she was diagnosed with pancreatic cancer. She fought it for many years and even survived for a short while after an operation at the University Hospital in Gainsville. She died in 1997 only 60 years old. I was happy, however, that a few years earlier I had been able to bring her to Germany to see her father in Leipzig. When the tough old man who had the kids walk two steps behind him, opened the door and saw Karin he broke down and cried.

I had never seen as much of Europe before as I did during these years with Roland although, truth be told, I had written guidebooks about it. I was rolling in a rented BMW at 100 miles per hour on Autobahns staying at George V in Paris, Ritz in Monaco, Amstel in Amsterdam, Frankfurter Hof in Frankfurt, Vier Jahreszeiten in Hamburg and the very British Browns at Albemarle Street in London.

The people who were running the pension funds and responsible for selecting the investment objects into which to funnel the employee's pension money were regular employees selected by their colleagues. Still, their responsibility did not mean that they were paid any more than their co-workers. They handled multi million dollars deals and ran funds that could be holding billions in assets, but hey did not make more than the rest of the guys in the office. We never met a client with a limo and driver. I picked them up at the airport in my three-year-old Volvo because you never knew who arrived by the same plane.

I must admit that I put them up at Fontainebleau Hilton but gave them a bill from our Holiday Inn hotels to attach to their list of travel expenses. Yes, and in Europe I wined and dined them and their wives maybe a bit too lavishly.

One of the advantages of my European travel was that I now and then could take a weekend in Sweden to visit my children and the growing number of grand children.

We often talked about my moving back to Sweden as I was closing in on retirement age. But it always came to "next time." One reason was that "the bunch", as I called my nine grand children, thought it was much better to have grandfather in Florida so they could visit him and Disney World at the same time. OK so Disney has sort of been a valid argument to stay here. The trouble is that now I suppose I have to stay on for the great grandchildren. As we say in Sweden, it does not matter how you turn, you always have your back behind you.

I was at the office on Ghoetestrasse in Frankfurt when Bruce Kaye called and said that he and his wife Debbie were going to Rome because she felt she could save a lot of money, enough even to pay for the trip, by buying the outfits for the season in Rome. Now he wanted me to come down to Rome to show them around because they had never been there before. They had as a matter of fact never been anywhere.

Bruce Kaye, one of the finest men I have ever had the honor to work for or with and call a friend, said to me: "You know Lars, I am running this big international outfit and I have never been anywhere, I don't even speak another language."

It takes guts and character to tell an employee a thing like that.

Now and then Bruce and I left Debbie in some shop

to have a drink or a cup of coffee. Then we had a bet on how much she had saved this time.

That was also when Bruce whether I, who know people everywhere might know some lady in Rome to make us four for dinner.

Yes, of course I knew Maria Resio-Persson, but that was so long ago, maybe fifteen years, maybe more. Would she see me? I doubted it, but she was in the phonebook at the same address. I called the old number I used to know so well.

"Hello, can I speak with Maria Resio?"

"You are speaking with her, Lars".

"It's like this, I am here... etc. etc. Will you dine with us?"

"I will ask my husband."

"Bring him along."

"That will be difficult because he lives in Naples."

I had met Maria when boarding a flight from Kennedy to Stockholm. She was stunning in a white ermine coat all the way down to her ankles. On board, oh miracle, she sat beside me. I was dumb struck. I wanted to say something but everything sounded so banal. I wanted to make a good impression.

Then, can you believe it? The Beauty started to talk to me! Then we talked without interruption for nine hours. We talked about music, theater, art, geography, history, cars, and bikes and ended up talking about the new Goss offset presses.

Maria's parents were Russian, so she spoke Russian. She went to school in Berlin, so she spoke German. The parents fled Hitler to Sweden where she studied at the Academy of Art and became solidly Swedish. She got a job as art director with J Walter Thompson in New York where she met and married an American officer who became military attaché in Rome where he died. She stayed on and worked as PR director for Hilton Hotels in the Mediterranean.

My wife met me at the airport and sounded very dry when I asked if we could drop Maria off on Norr Mälarstrand where her brother lived. He worked at the daily paper Dagens Nyheter.

In the years that went by whenever I was in Italy I looked her up. Yes, we had a romance.

I picked her up at the old address and we went to the hotel to meet the Kayes. When Maria saw Bruce in that black T-shirt under the elegant jacket that Don Johnson had launched as a fashion on TV in the U.S., she asked:

"Are you going out like that?" When he said yes, she said "Not with me."

"What did I tell you," said Debbie.

After dinner we went to Maria's place for a nightcap. It was all so familiar. Bruce went into her library and looked through albums with Maria hosting dignitaries as Hilton's PR manager.

"Where is Lars?" asked Bruce.

"He is there," said Maria and pointed to a bookshelf where she had my books, a flower and a picture.

Debbie, this Jewish straight talker, just looked at me and said: "You bastard."

From that moment and from Maria's rejection of Bruce's dinner attire developed a life long friendship between these two women.

A contact in Geneva called me in Miami to be prepared to take care of a client of his, a monsieur Marcel Rivera who wanted to find an apartment in Miami. He only spoke French and Spanish so Miami suited him best.

Roland was part owner with the billionaire Muss family of the four condominium Towers of Quayside Miami. Mr. Rivera bought a $411,000 penthouse for himself and his family and another apartment for his brother for $265,000. He paid cash.

Marcel Rivera did not look like a rich influential man. He looked more like a construction worker who had carried bricks on his back up buildings all his life.

Exiting Quayside, two apartments wealthier, Marcel Rivera said he needed some lighter wear because it was frying hot. I suggested some nice men's shops downtown. But Marcel saw a K-Mart across the street and said it would do. He bought a T-shirt, a pair of polyester shorts and a pair of sneakers and the whole purchase did no even come to fifty dollars.

He changed in the car and then asked if I thought he could go to Credit Suisse like that. I told him that his money, not his pants were all that mattered to the bank. The girl at the reception looked at him and wrinkled her nose, as deodorant was not yet very popular in Europe. I told her that Mr. Rivera was here to see the manager. We sat down and waited. After twenty minutes I thought we had waited long enough and she'd better get the manager NOW! She called the manager, which I don't think she had done before. He came out bowing almost to the floor and said that Geneva had been in touch with him to prepare for his visit. He did not notice how Rivera was dressed.

After visiting the bank Rivera and I went to McDonalds for a hamburger. I asked him if there was anything else I could do for him as I had some very interesting subjects and objects. He replied that he could hear about it later but now he had a couple of agents to see. Prearranged, he said.

That's when I asked him how come he spoke French with a pied noir accent (the term refers to French colonists of Algeria).

"Parce que je suis pied noir." he answered.

When I asked him where in Algeria he came from he said, just a small place called Oujda between Oran and Colomb Bechar far out in the bush. "But how come monsieur Ottoson knows so much about Algeria?"

"Oh, I said, is that big fig tree still outside the city hall in Oujda?"

"Mon Dieu! Where else have you been?"

I told him how we had traveled to Colomb Bechar and at Beni bel Abbes where we had left the road for some agricultural project where we could fill our jerry cans with water for the Sahara crossing.

"Mon Dieu! That's my parents' place! That's where I was born! So what else is it that you wanted to talk to me about and show me?"

When Algeria, like other French colonies in Africa, became independent from France in 1962, thousands of colony-born Frenchmen returned to France. They sold what they could and just left the rest. Rivera's family settled in southern France in the area of Aix en Provence.

Marcel Rivera felt that everyone who knew some trade or had a profession left the colonies and thus, there must exist a tremendous need for professional people. So Rivera filled a ship with sacks of cement and sailed to Gabon, a small country between Kongo and Cameroon. He got work right away to build offices for the government, including a palace for the president and a hotel. He built almost the entire capital of Libreville. The country was one of the most peaceful and stable in Africa thanks to its off shore oil production. While many entrepreneurs had difficulties to get paid in Africa, Rivera had no problem. He found a way for the International Monetary Fund to pay for most projects. They paid the money to his bank in Switzerland. He kept a one-room office in Geneva with one assistant. He went there for his private financial transactions and to transfer money to his working bank in Libreville. When in Geneva he slept in the office. He made sure that also other international support organizations that sponsored projects in Gabon paid his bank in Switzerland. Slow and steady

Rivera became a very rich man. He married a tall good looking local girl and had twin girls with her. He sent the girls to the finest private schools in Switzerland.

I helped Rivera to buy some water front properties in Coconut Grove, two lots on the bay on Key Biscayne, a small shopping center on US1 and an office block on Biscayne Boulevard in Miami. Rivera did not want to invest his money in France. He wanted it all in Miami. He had around 1985 only one property left in Gabon, a big hotel in the center of the city.

The president of Gabon wanted to buy the hotel and a price of $4 million was agreed upon. After all had been signed and sealed, Marcel Rivera told me that the president Omar Bongo gave him a check for $4,000,000 drawn on a bank account in Switzerland which fit Rivera like a glove. The trouble was, however, that the check bounced. There was no money in the account.

Rivera took off to Gabon with his lawyer to straighten it all out. The problem was that they could not find anyone in Gabon to help them. Like a Gabon attorney said: "If I sign on against the president I might just as well sign my own death sentence."

While assisting Rivera with his many Miami deals and acquisitions the partnership of Robins and Friedland closed down Roland International. They had made enough money and wanted to go fishing. Rivera and I founded a corporation, Investus International to handle his affairs in the U.S.. We rented a small office in Coral Gables and set out to find some project, which we could develop and manage. The Coconut Grove land and the lots on Key Biscayne were, so to say, already spoken for and not in our hands.

We decided on something that would encompass a rather big slice of land in close proximity to Disneyworld and meeting some Disney needs - an upscale recreational vehicle park, badly needed by some visitors on wheels. We launched the TRAILINN RV Country Club. We aimed it at visitors with larger motor homes and joined an organization in Washington DC that allowed members of one park to use another member park elsewhere in the USA. Called the Camp Coast to Coast it was an organization of hundreds of similar parks around the country. You would be allowed to park for a dollar a night during two separate weeks a year, and twice two weeks a year in your home park. We soon had over a thousand members and a healthy cash flow and no loans. The land was paid for. We gave our members more than just electricity and water and drainage. We provided phone and TV.

Trail Inn covered about 400 acres with clubhouse, two Olympic size pools, tennis courts, and three laundry buildings.

Of course, our location on Lake Davenport was ideal, two miles from Disney on the main artery to the Disney area where Route 194 empties like a hotel corridor into north-south highway25.

We were in a project that craved millions and so far, Rivera paid everything cash. The only negative about the location was that our acres were located in four different counties: Orange, Polk, Lake and Seminole. That meant four permits and four inspectors for each permit. First you had to have all permits and licenses ready from the local community. Then you had to clear the county and then with the State. Every one of these had a special inspector. Different subjects were e.g. drainage, ground usage, environmental issues, drilling, etc. We had to set aside a room in the sales building for the exclusive use by the inspectors. Then we had to hire a special engineer to take care of the inspectors.

Here is an example. To build the entrance road to the park we had to cross a five feet wide ditch, The ditch was regarded as environmentally sensitive and we were not allowed to touch it - unless of course we set aside ten times that amount of land somewhere else as compensation.

Lake Davenport is an idyllic little lake, about half a mile long and a quarter of a mile wide. It is ideal for simple fishing, water skiing and canoeing. When the state inspector saw that we intended to build a small dock for the canoes, he became alarmed. The Corps of Engineers in Washington DC is the entity responsible for all waterways in the US. We had to provide aerial views of the entire lake and close ups of the dock sites. We entertained a helicopter crew on this project for two days. Still no definite approval. I was back to "follow the law to the letter". Skip building a dock. A floating platform is allowed. Lets' make one and tie it to a couple of trees or poles in the ground. It worked!

What was it that the Corps of Engineers wanted in Washington? They wanted a complete drawing of the dock we intended to build. They needed the aerial views to show the surrounding area and then, in increment, down to the site of the dock. They asked for an analysis of the vegetation and an expert's analysis of the water life in the lake. As I said some time it pays to follow the law by the letter. We built the floating platform.

The French and Swedish, American and Floridian flags marked the entrance to Trail Inn showing that we were open for business. Or were we? A congressman up in Tallahassee, Florida's capital seemed to think that we should not be. And neither should other projects of a similar kind. As long as we were under construction we should escrow membership fees, he said. And not only that, the developer should pay into a non-withdrawal escrow account a sum equal to the construction costs. Something like that was unheard of so when the senator from Lake County called and said: "How do you propose to handle this situation, Mr. Ottoson?"

I answered "What situation?"

He told me about the suggested law that now only needed to be approved in the Senate the last week in May 1986 to kill the project. To start with, he gave me a rather cold shoulder. When I explained that we already had millions in this project but that we could of course abandon it, fire about a fifty workers from his county and hurt several suppliers he started to listen. After all, the unemployment rate in Lake County was already a problem. Finally he said:

"I shall see what I can do. I understand this is a serious issue for the region. But I need something that would motivate my colleagues in the Senate to kill the issue".

"Would by any chance fifty thousand dollars be helpful?"

"Oh yes, that would help a lot."

We were already a week into May so I had some nervous days. We were finally only four hours from the senate to close for the season. I had already chewed over every possible alternative many times and talked with everybody from the chairwoman to the labor union rep when the phone finally rang half an hour before the Senate closed for the season.

A happy senator could not keep his voice down when he said

"We killed it Lars! We killed the son-of-a-bitch! With 40 session minutes left. Last issue. Thanks to you the GOP has no longer a mortgage on its office building in Tallahassee."

Everyone who donated something of value to the Republican Party in Florida got a plaque in a given place in the party headquarters. The donor then had to name for instance a room after a president. I suggested George H. W. Bush for the conference room. When told that he was not a president, I said "But he will be." So there it was on the door, a plaque saying:

*The George W Bush Conference Room,
donated by Lars H. Ottoson.*

I have not been up there for a long time to see if it is still there. Anyway, I liked the old man even more as a person than as a politician.

It was not long before GOP's finance guru in Florida, Alec Courtelis had me on his private plane going here and there as a motivational speaker - the happy immigrant story about the American dream.

Ronald Reagan was president and the word about my - or rather Trail Inn's generosity reached Washington and suddenly I was having dinner at the White House.

I don't think the street entrance guards had seen a White House tuxedoed dinner guest arriving on foot before my attendance for a dinner. I came alone because at the time Karin was spending time in Germany with her ailing father.

All guests mingled waiting in the big music salon for the President and Mrs. Reagan to arrive. When we heard Hail the Chief and the Master of Ceremony announced the arrival of the President and Mrs. Reagan, we were already in a waiting line to be received. A Marin Corps Major by the side of the presidential couple asked your name to be forwarded to the President. When it was my turn and the Major heard I was Swedish he said his name was Olson and that his father was from the district of Dalsland and so he put in a few extra words about me to the President. That in turn made the President seek me out later in the Blue Room. I was at a so-called intimate dinner for about fifty guests. I remember that I shared a table with a guy who owned the San Francisco 49-ers. I was one of the few single men at the party and had been given a White House lady to accompany me and fill out the seating at the table of ten.

The dinner consisted of lobster soup, Poularde a la Derby with fresh asparagus, three kinds of salad and as desert a cherry soufflé. We drank Kistler Chardonnay 1986, Saintsbury Pinot Noir 1985 and Schramsberg Cremant Demi Sec 1983.

I treasured the autographed menu for which I can thank my dinner companion. I mean in the White House you just don't run up to the President's table and ask for autographs.

After the dinner we withdrew to the Blue Room to mingle. The President came over to me and talked informally longer than with anyone else, most likely because what Major Olson had told him when introducing me. He wanted to know why I had come to the U.S. after a TV career in Sweden. He knew talking to me that I had been cleared both by the CIA and the FBI because without their clearance you haven't got a chance to dine in the White House.

Of course an unconventional after dinner conversation with a president of the United States is never unconventional. It is basically an exchange of niceties.

When it started to be too crowded around us Reagan's eyes caught Nancy's who then moved in gracefully like no aide could.

On the campaign trail I came to meet George H W Bush many times in Florida and campaign a bit with Senator Paula Hawkins. Whenever a party finds someone who has contributed to the cause, they don't let go. There are so many levels in which contributors are categorized and all are ranked according to the $ amount contributed. The finest level is of course where you receive personal letters from the presidential candidate. Dear Lars, It was so nice to see you again etc. etc. Then comes, as in my case. The Florida Victory Committee, The Inaugural Committee, Senatorial Inner Circle, The President's Club, The President's Round Table, The President's Inner Circle etc. etc.

Especially the President's Inner Circle is very exclusive. I was told that I shared the President's attention with greats like Sam Walton, Estee Lauder, beer tycoon Joe Coors and Arnold Schwarzenegger. Of course other presidents and presidential candidates have other names for their support groups, but essentially whatever you call them, they are all the same and established for the same reasons.

The last thing I heard from GOP before Clinton took over was an invitation to attend the inauguration of The Ronald Regan Presidential Library in California. But apparently I was not forgotten. I suddenly received an invitation to The President's Dinner on May 21, 2003. Father Bush and Barbara sent the invitation saying: Many of our party leaders are looking forward to seeing you again. Of course, at the price of $25,00 a table or $2,500 a plate. I considered it for a while and then decided to pass that time.

The ironic thing is that I like the older Bush but I can't say I am a republican. I can't say I am a Democrat either. I shelled out some money when I needed a favor.

I am still involved in following politics in Sweden. I am sort of semi anchored in the Swedish political system. Not because I agree with it all but because I have three children who are living with it.

SWEDISH AMERICA

I have over the years in Florida taken a strong interest in promoting Sweden and "swedishness," vigorously pursuing every chance to promote the country of my birth.

Together with an old friend from Stocksund, Lars Hummerhielm, once chairman of Sweden's Young Conservatives and for the role like the Bad Boy Ruda in a children's movie series. He was actually a real baron whose forefather the general fought with Karl XII in Russia against Peter the Great.

In 1992 we activated a slumbering Swedish American Chamber of Commerce and within five years it had as many members as the hitherto biggest Chamber, the one in New York that had been around since 1907.

It was released from an embryo placed by Kerstin Williams, who was of Swedish advertising stock. We had an office with three interns at magnificent Coral Gables Landmark, Biltmore Hotel where Hummerhielm ruled under the first chairman Anders Ahltin of Ahltin Medical and then under Captain Nils G. Nord, a captains' captain and ruler of the cruise giant, the Royal Caribbean Line.

SACC Florida was for ten years the most active Swedish Chamber in America with exhibitions, seminars, conventions, debates and sister city exchanges with Stockholm County. Its then mayor Ulf Adolfsson became a frequent guest in Miami. Our Lucia celebrations drew a thousand to the church in Coral Gables. I traveled the state as a speaker for SACC from Miami to Jacksonville up north and everywhere I found the Swedish business pulse pounding. I gathered it all in a 16-24 page Newsletter six times a year. At the Biltmore we ran a Swedish exhibition with over a hundred companies and towns.

Lars Hummerhielm had an unusual gift to get people together. When the Swedish community lost him to a stroke in 1999, he was working on getting the King of Sweden over for a visit. He had also just founded the Association of Binational Chambers of Commerce (AB-iCC). He was a lover of classical music, a glass of wine, a good cigar and his wife Sheryl, who was a staunch business director. She came to be finance head for what was left of General Development.

Karl G. Stenström took over after Nils G. Nordh. He was the guy that had done the splitting up of the Swedish Match conglomerate and sold it not once but twice. He had secured a fortune for himself through one of the sales, a management buy out, and moved to a multi million-dollar villa on the water on Key Biscayne. Over here he introduced the Swedish Pergo flooring to the U.S. market and it is said to be the market leader today. He also bought and renovated one of the old art deco hotels on South Beach. I have sat there many times dining on its veranda watching the exhibitionists walk past exposing their butts, tits and steroid enhanced body work.

As a young man Kålle, as Stenström is known, worked for many years in Latin America. One of his tennis partners became Florida's future governor and presidential brother Jeb Bush. When Sweden's former Prime Minister and future Secretary of State, Carl Bildt had a problem to fully understand the school voucher system used in Florida and needed some practical information he got together with Jeb Bush at Kålle's place.

As I involved myself writing about Swedish business and events, I stumbled on a fascinating Swedish past in Florida. It happened one day in the city of Sanford when I read a street sign saying Upsala Road. I followed it and came to a little white church - New Upsala Swedish Episcopalian Church. Here once was a town called New Upsala founded in 1872 by 400 Swedes recruited in Sweden by a general Sanford who wanted reliable Swedish workers for his big citrus plantation. He turned to a judge, Lars Henschen in the university city of Uppsala. His two sons helped to recruit all the labor for his undertaking. They sailed from Gothenburg in May of 1871. One of the Henschen brothers was somehow involved with the foundation of the Swedish American periodical Nordstjernan in 1872. It has been published ever since.

I stood there in the city museum in Sanford, in the town once named New Upsala and read the 400 names of the Swedes who came here to work for the wages of a five acre plot and some measly pay. What happened to them then?

They may not have been here if it was not for a teenaged sailor, Johan Anders Boström, originally of the island of Gotland in the Baltic, who shipwrecked off the Florida coast in 1855. He started to cultivate the wild oranges as he dared to work in the bush despite the Seminole war. He became one of the fathers of the American citrus industry and founded the cities of Ormond Beach and Daytona Beach. When his oranges after a dozen years started to reach the north, he was the one to inspire Sanford. And Swedes came from all corners to start citrus plantations. It was said that in 1880 every citrus plantation from coast to coast was owned, worked or

Illustration: Gunnulf Björkman

managed by Swedes. In the process they also founded St. Petersburg and Hallandale and had a lot to do with establishing Florida's economy. I would say their influence was paramount.

No one state in the U.S. has been more industrially influenced by a single nationality than Florida by the Swedes. They founded the citrus industry when there was nothing else in that southern state since cotton had failed. They rode it to success and dominance. And by the way, Disney World is built on an Olof Larsson's old citrus groves. And by the way again, Arnold Lindberg from Jönköping built it - an old friend of Walt Disney from days they were nobodies and the foresighted Axel Wenner-Gren built the first Monorail for the development. But I am saving all that historical Swedish stuff for another book. I fear that if I don't write it, it won't be written and an important part of Swedish immigration history maybe lost forever.

TO BE CONTINUED...

I found the typewriter again about fifteen years ago, started work on new books and contribute a column to every issue of Nordstjernan, the Swedish American New York based periodical where I also acted as Editor in Chief for a little over a year. My work for Nordstjernan and the Swedish American Chamber of Commerce inspired the latter to honor me with a Swede of the Year award for "Contributions to the Swedish community in Florida" in 2005. It has been an honor and a privilege to live and to contribute.

I never ended up in a one bedroom on my beloved Stockholm's Östermalm, neither did I retire to a golf course somewhere in my beloved Florida. I am still at it, working on my next book and the next column. See you soon.

Lars Henrik Ottoson
Vero Beach, Florida, 2009

LARS-HENRIK OTTOSON

SACC

The Swedish American Chamber of Commerce of Florida

cordially invites you to its

2005 ANNUAL GALA DINNER

featuring

WINNER of the SACC AWARD TO THE
SWEDE OF THE YEAR
LARS OTTOSON

For his outstanding long term contribution to SACC and the Swedish Community in Florida.

Wednesday, May 11, 20005, at 7.00 p.m.
The Ritz-Carlton Hotel
3300 SW 27th Avenue, Coconut Grove, FL33133

RESERVATIONS
must be made latest Thursday May 5, by sending your name, telephone number, and number of people in your group, by email to: sacc@sacc.florida.com
Fee: $68 per person by check only (no credit cards), must be mailed to::
Your reservation will only be confirmed once your check has arrived!
NO EXCEPTIONS1 NO TELEPHONE RESERVATIONS1
Dress Code: Black tie (Dark suit optional), Cocktail Dress

SPONSORED BY:

LARS-HENRIK OTTOSON

INDEX
(of people I met)

ABBA 203, 213
Abd el Krim 128
Ahlquist, Edwin 205
Andersson, Arne 58
Andersson, Benny 9 211
Andersson, Stickan 210
Attawel Ibrahim 133
Attawel Kadri 134
Backman, Pierre 70
Bannister, Everett 233
Bergman, Ingmar, 49 37 43
Björklund, Olle 191
Björling, Jussi 93
Björn, Hasse 168
Blom, Svea 142
Bonnier, Abbe 12
Bonnier, Simon 222
Bowe, Nigel 227
Bratt, Hasse
Brøndum, Otto 92 93 100
Bush, George H. W., ex pres USA 261
Christensson, Henry 191
Christie, Harold Sir 223 230
Coakley, Livingstone 227
Collin, Claes
Cosell Howard 205
Cronstrand, Börje 58
Crusner, Lennart 203
Danielsson, Bengt 61
Davis Jr, Sammy 104
Dellert, Kjerstin 59
Derkert, Lars
Erlander, Tage 108
Ehrling, Sixten 93
Eklöf, Rudolf "R:et" 57
Engelbrecht, Jacobus 176

Engström, Gert 55
Eriksson, Agne 26
Eriksson, Annalisa 102
Eriksson, Karl 143
Essén, Ingemar 12 39 40
Franke, Gösta 39
Furugård, Birger 49
Gallay, George 174
Git Gay 36
Grive, Bengt
Grunander, Arne
Grut, Wille 46
Grotte, Ole 110
Gullers, K.W.
Goering, Hermann 81 82
Göring, Hermann 81 82
Hadarsson, Hadar 60
Hagander, Vera 29
Hagander, Hugo "Loppan" 29
Halldén, Nalle 63
Hallström, Bengt 70
Haskel, Joel 12 49 214
Hassner, Rune
Heath Edward Brit. PM 89
Hemingway, Ernest 162
Hep Stars 210
Hess, Rudolf 81
Horner, A. Wing Com. 87 89
Hyland, Lennart 73
Hägg, Gunder 58
Jackson, Robert US Prosecuor 174
Johansson, Ingemar 201 203
Johansson de Malleray, Anne-Mari 117
Josephsson, Erland 9 42 44
Jumper, Moses 244
Jungstedt, Torsten 70 72

Kaye, Bruce 251
Keen, A.F. Mayir Cape Town
Kjellin, Alf 39 98 241
Kjellström, Nils
Klint, Barbro 104
Kohler, René 120
Kolming, Britt 74
Komstedt, Leo 113
Lacroix, Mme 176
Langer, Pecka 12 204
Larsson-Kramer, Britt
Leadbetter, C Cons. 64 65
Livijn, Claes 92 106
Lidman, Håkan 56
Linde, Ulf Prof. 59
Lindholm, Sven Olof 49
Lindström, Bengt 109 113 169
Linnér, Sture 192
Lucas, A Dr. 174
Lumumba, Patrice Zaire PM 145
Maersk-Möller 226
Magnuson, Frank 217
Mannberg, Bernhard 222 231
Marmstedt, Lorens 168
Masters, Karin
Medina, Jean de 147 174
Mikes, George 69
Mitchum, Robert 228
Ndumanya 138
Nilsson, Johan MP 55
Nilsson, Tore 12 57
Niven, David 85
Nygren, Varg Olle 62
Nykvist, Sven 9 36 167
Oakes, Harry, Sir 224
Olson, Emma Lou 244
Olsson, Folke 222 228
Olsson, Gits 12
Olsson, Halvor William 70
Pallin, Ingemar 42
Palm, Roland 109 113 194
Persson, Edvard 22
Persson, Finn
Persson, Gustav 29
Petré, Gio 174

Pindlling, Lyndon 229
Ponti, Carlo 102
Pryzelius, Gösta 9 12 42 214
Putnam, Patrik 149 172
Ramel, Povel 29 43 95
Resio (Persson), Maria 254
Rat Pack 104
Reynolds, Burt 105
Risberg, Olle boxer 206
Rivera, Marcel 255
Ros, Edmundo 75
Rosenberg, Hilding, Prof 37
Samuelsson, Rickard 222
Sandberg, Birger "Farsan"
Sandrew, Anders 26 35
Sands, Stafford, Sir 223
Scientology 247
Schultz, Karin (DN) 71
Sjöblom, Alice Babs
Sjöström, Henning 9 214
Skoglar, Ester 142
Smet, Martine de 172
Smith, George A 233
Stensland, Lisbeth 105
Stevens, Inger, Actress 105
Strandberg, Lennart 56
Strandberg, Olle
Söderberg A. Missionär 154
Söderqvist, Åke 192 196
Taberer C, Game warden 161
"Tarzan" 149
Thunborg, Olof. Amb. 63
Turner, Robert 199
Unsgård, Håkan 70
Vought, Allan 55
Wachenfeldt, Bertil von 62
Wally, Gustav 97
Wenner-Gren, Axel 223 268
Westin, Gunnar 244
Wickbom, T.G. 73
Wilkens, May Britt 103
Windsor, Duke of 223
Wretman, Thore
Østvik, Ørjan 111

www.ingramcontent.com/pod-product-compliance
Lightning Source LLC
Chambersburg PA
CBHW071654090426
42738CB00009B/1518